Out of
Business and
On Budget

Out of
Business and
On Budget

The Challenge of
Military Financing in Indonesia

Lex Rieffel

Jaleswari Pramodhawardani

UNITED STATES-INDONESIA SOCIETY

BROOKINGS INSTITUTION PRESS
Washington, D.C.

Copyright © 2007
THE BROOKINGS INSTITUTION
1775 Massachusetts Avenue, N.W., Washington, D.C. 20036
www.brookings.edu

Library of Congress Cataloging-in-Publication data
Rieffel, Alexis, 1941–
  Out of business and on budget : the challenge of military financing in Indonesia / Lex Rieffel and Jaleswari Pramodhawardani.
      p.   cm.
  Summary: "Describes the evolution of the military's business empire and its decline after 1998. Examines what is necessary to bring the Indonesian military "on-budget": what policies are required, what Indonesia can learn from other nations, and what a realistic timetable looks like"—Provided by publisher.
  Includes bibliographical references and index.
  ISBN-13: 978-0-8157-7447-1 (pbk. : alk. paper)
  ISBN-10: 0-8157-7447-8 (pbk. : alk. paper)
  1. National security—Economic aspects—Indonesia. 2. Indonesia—Economic policy. 3. National security—Indonesia. 4. Indonesia—Military policy. 5. Indonesia. Tentara Nasional. I. Pramodhawardani, Jaleswari. II. Title.
  HC450.D4R54 2007
  338.4'7355009598—dc22   2007015828

1 3 5 7 9 8 6 4 2

The paper used in this publication meets minimum requirements of the American National Standard for Information Sciences—Permanence of Paper for Printed Library Materials: ANSI Z39.48-1992.

Typeset in Minion

Composition by Peter Lindeman
Arlington, Virginia

Printed by Victor Graphics
Baltimore, Maryland

Contents

Part III: The Way Forward

Appendixes

Foreword

The United States-Indonesia Society, USINDO, is pleased to sponsor *Out of Business and On Budget: The Challenge of Military Financing in Indonesia*. Over the years there has been great public interest, not only in Indonesia but also in the United States and elsewhere, in the role of the Indonesian Armed Forces (TNI) in the economy and the operation of its money-making enterprises.

Redefining the role of the TNI and providing the budget support required to carry out this role is one of the most complex challenges facing the government of President Susilo Bambang Yudhoyono. We believe that this fresh and comprehensive treatment of the TNI's business activities and financing requirements will help to inform the ongoing debate about the future of the TNI.

While the present study leaves a number of questions unanswered, the authors highlight the many steps that will have to be taken to decrease and ultimately end the TNI's reliance on off-budget financing and to achieve the degree of budget transparency expected under democratic governance. Many stakeholders, including the Indonesian House of Representatives (DPR), have an interest in the orderly and democratic transformation of the armed forces into a more capable, operationally effective, and well-supported institution.

USINDO is grateful to the authors, Lex Rieffel and Jaleswari Pramodhawardani, for their diligence and constructive approach to this important aspect of building a just, prosperous, and democratic society in Indonesia. Our hope is that the contribution to scholarship and policymaking represented by *Out of Business and On Budget* will spur further reform in the defense sector. The views expressed herein are those of the authors, however, and do not necessarily represent those of the United States-Indonesia Society and its trustees.

ALPHONSE F. LA PORTA
President, United States-
Indonesia Society
Washington, D.C.
May 2007

Acknowledgments

The United States-Indonesia Society (USINDO) invited us to undertake this study in mid-2005, although it had in mind a smaller book and a much earlier delivery date. USINDO President Alphonse La Porta created the political space for the project and Congressional and Defense Relations Officer Donald Eirich made sure the support we needed materialized. Their colleagues in USINDO's Washington and Jakarta offices provided critical logistical help.

At the Brookings Institution, Lael Brainard, vice president and director, Global Economy and Development, enabled us to use the facilities of this great institution, including its outstanding library. At the Brookings Institution Press, Chris Kelaher was the study's first fan and never wavered each time our planned completion date slipped another month. Janet Walker, Susan Woollen, Larry Converse, and others put the manuscript on the fastest possible track for publication.

At the Indonesian Institute, we are grateful to Executive Director Jeffry Geovanie for providing well-situated office space and efficient staff support. Pak Soegeng and Sukardi Rinakit at Soegeng Sarjadi Syndicate also offered outstanding hospitality on short notice.

We received exceptional help from three sources in Jakarta. Juwono Sudarsono, minister of defense, welcomed our effort and made it possible to have productive interviews with senior officials in the ministry, notably with Secretary General Lieutenant General Sjaffrie Sjamsoeddin. When we began the study, Endriartono Sutarto, TNI commander, gave us an early opportunity to explain our study, and other senior officers in TNI headquarters arranged several key briefings for us, especially Brigadier General Bibit Santoso at the

Information Center. Our deepest debt, however, is to Jakarta's leading experts on military reform, who provided us with an abundance of information and insight. They included Agus Widjojo, Andi Widjajanto, Bilveer Singh, Dewi Fortuna Anwar, Edy Prasetyono, Ikrar Nusa Bhakti, Indria Samego, J. Kristiadi, Kusnanto Anggoro, Marcus Mietzner, Rizal Sukma, Salim Said, Sukardi Rinakit, and Tatik Hafidz.

We also interviewed dozens of people in Jakarta and Washington who made substantial contributions to our work. Among these were active and retired TNI officers, active and retired officials in other Indonesian ministries (especially the Ministry of Finance), members of the DPR, think tank experts, businessmen, lawyers, NGO representatives, media personalities, officials in multilateral institutions, foreign advisers, U.S. government officials, and current and former defense attachés. Their strong encouragement kept us going in the face of exceptional obstacles. Finally, the comments we received from four reviewers of our first draft enabled us to restructure and strengthen our study substantially, and we are most grateful to them.

We can only hope that our study meets the expectations of this remarkable group of supporters. Of course we alone bear responsibility for the analysis, the conclusions, and the organization of this study.

Words and Abbreviations

ABRI	Angkatan Bersenjata Republik Indonesia (Indonesian Armed Forces; in use before 1999)
ADMM	ASEAN Defense Ministers' Meeting
APBN	Anggaran Pendapatan Belanja Negara (national budget)
APEC	Asia-Pacific Economic Cooperation
ARF	ASEAN Regional Forum
ASEAN	Association of Southeast Asian Nations
Bappenas	Badan Perencanaan Pembangunan Nasional (National Development Planning Board)
BKR	Badan Keamanan Rakyat (People's Security Corps)
BPK	Badan Pemeriksa Keuangan (Supreme Audit Board)
BP MIGAS	Badan Pelaksana Kegiatan Usaha Hulu Minyak Bumi (Executive Agency for Upstream Oil and Gas Activity)
BRR	Badan Rehabilitasi dan Rekonstruksi (Agency for the Rehabilitation and Reconstruction of the Region and Community of Aceh and Nias)
BULOG	Badan Urusan Logistik (state logistics agency)
BUMN	Badan Usaha Milik Negara (state-owned enterprises)
CADEK	Catur Darma Eka Karma (four duties one purpose)
CGI	Consultative Group for Indonesia
CIFOR	Center for International Forestry Research
DPN	Dewan Pertahanan Nasional (National Defense Council)
DPR	Dewan Perwakilan Rakyat (House of Representatives)
Dwifungsi	Dual functions
GAM	Gerakan Aceh Merdeka (Free Aceh Movement)
Golkar	Golongan karya (functional group; name of political party)
Hansip	Pertahanan sipil (civil defense organization)
IBRA	Indonesian Bank Restructuring Agency

Kamra	Keamanan rakyat (People's Security Organization)
KKN	Korupsi, kolusi dan nepotisme (corruption, collusion, and nepotism)
KNIL	Koninklijk Nederlands Indisch Leger (Royal Netherlands East Indies Army)
Kodahan	Komando daerah pertahanan (area defense command)
Kodam	Komando daerah militer (regional military command)
Kodim	Komando distrik militer (district military command)
Kopassus	Komando Pasukan Khusus (army special forces)
Kopkamtib	Komando Operasi Pemulihan Keamanan dan Ketertiban (Operational Command for the Restoration of Security and Order)
Korem	Komando resort militer (military command post)
Kowilhan	Komando Wilayah Pertahanan (Regional Defense Command)
Kostrad	Komando Strategis Angkatan Darat (Army Strategic Reserves Command)
KPLP	Kesatuan Penjagaan Laut dan Pantai (Coast and Sea Guard Unit)
LEMHANAS	Lembaga Pertahanan Nasional (National Resilience Institute)
LIPI	Lembaga Ilmu Pengetahuan Indonesia (National Institute of Sciences)
MPR	Majelis Perwakilan Rakyat (People's Consultative Assembly)
NKRI	Negara Kesatuan Republik Indonesia (Unitary State of the Republic of Indonesia)
Pancasila	Five principles (Indonesia's national ideology)
PDI-P	Partai Demokrasi Indonesia-Perjuangan (Democratic Party of Indonesia of Struggle)
PKB	Partai Kebangkitan Bangsa (National Awakening Party)
PKI	Partai Komunis Indonesia (Indonesian Communist Party)
Polri	Polisi Republic Indonesia (National Police)
SBY	Susilo Bambang Yudhoyono (president of Indonesia)
Seskoad	Sekolah Staf dan Komando Angkatan Darat (Army Staff and Command School)
SIPRI	Stockholm International Peace Research Institute
TNI	Tentara Nasional Indonesia (Indonesian Armed Forces; in use since 1999)
TRIDEK	Tri Dharma Eka Putra (three missions one deed)
TSTB TNI	Tim Supervisi Transformasi Bisnis TNI (TNI Business Takeover Team)
Wanra	Perlawan rakyat (People's Resistance Organization)
YKPP	Yayasan Kesejahteraan Perumahan Prajurit (Foundation for Soldiers Housing)

1

Policy Objectives: Out of Business and On Budget

Indonesia has been called the world's largest unknown country. Certainly few Americans can locate it geographically. Even fewer know that it has a population of almost 250 million, exceeded only by China, India, and the United States. Images that come to mind relate to Aceh's devastation after the tsunami of December 2004, Bali's picturesque beaches and rice paddies, the recent spate of terrorist bombings, gamelan music, batik textiles, the Borobudur temple, the flamboyant President Sukarno, and the "Smiling General," President Suharto.

The image we would like to start with is hard to capture. It is Indonesia's remarkable transition—beginning in 1998—to a democratic society. For a country that only declared independence from Dutch colonial rule in 1945, suffered seven years of turbulence under a parliamentary democracy, and then endured thirty years of authoritarian rule under Suharto, the progress made since 1998 in building a viable democratic political system has been phenomenal and surprising.[1] An especially auspicious achievement was the 2004 election of Susilo Bambang Yudhoyono (also known as SBY) as president by more votes than any other world leader has received, including George W. Bush less than six weeks later.[2]

The success or failure of Indonesia's second experiment with democracy may well depend on its armed forces, the Tentara Nasional Indonesia (TNI), widely considered to be the strongest institution in the country. It was Indonesian military units, not civilian politicians like Sukarno, that won the war of independence against the Dutch, prevented the Communist Party from tak-

1. See Rieffel (2004).
2. Susilo Bambang Yudhoyono received 67.2 million votes, George W. Bush 62.0 million.

1

ing over in the 1960s, and created the political stability undergirding the rapid economic growth and reduction of poverty in the 1970s and 1980s. More to the point of this study, the TNI has not fully embraced the concept of civilian supremacy because the country's civilian politicians are widely viewed as incompetent and the bureaucrats as corrupt. Many officers and large segments of society harbor visions of the TNI regaining its preeminent role in the political and economic life of the country.

Two basic factors contribute to the tension between the vibrant but immature civil society that has emerged since 1998 and the military establishment, which is not large in numbers but appears to be more coherent than any other social group. One is the existence of a vast range of off-budget revenue-generating activities that make it possible for the TNI to act independently of the government. The other is popular pressure, reinforced by sixty years of history, to keep the military's share of the central government budget low—6.3 percent in 2007, equivalent to 0.9 percent of GDP. Our study focuses on both factors, which are really two sides of the same coin.

Purposes of the Study

The immediate purpose of our study is to assemble in a single source the basic information required to understand the policy challenges for the Indonesian government in the narrow area of winding down the TNI's business activities and in the broad area of putting the TNI on full budget funding. Although business activities have played an important part in the life of the Indonesian Armed Forces from the moment Sukarno and other nationalist leaders declared the nation's independence from colonial rule by the Netherlands in 1945, the first major study of these activities did not appear until 1998.[3] Since then the subject has been taken up in more than half a dozen books published in English and in Bahasa Indonesia (the official language of Indonesia), as well as in dozens of academic papers, short opinion pieces, and in-depth press reports. Rather than attempt to produce new historical or empirical information, we have built our study on the wealth of information that is already available.

By highlighting the complexity of pursuing reforms in this area, we hope the Indonesian public will more clearly see why it will be difficult to make meaningful progress here in the next two to three years. Equally important, we hope that policymakers in Indonesia will gain a better idea of fruitful steps to be taken, and that foreign governments eager to assist Indonesia in con-

---

3. Samego and others (1998).

solidating democratic governance will be able to target their concerns more sensibly and contribute support in more effective forms.

Our study differs from preceding ones primarily in that it looks forward more than backward. It is not a historical or investigative study but a policy analysis focusing on thirty issues inextricably linked to the process of weaning the TNI from its many sources of off-budget revenue and putting the TNI fully on budget (box 1-1). The government's challenge here can be likened to an algebra problem. It takes three simultaneous equations to solve a problem with three unknowns. In this case, however, there are thirty unknowns. Inevitably, the related policy decisions made with respect to the thirty issues will have to be sequenced. Making them all at once is not feasible. As a consequence, the benefits of making sensible choices may not be visible until a "tipping point" is reached well along the way and momentum develops to carry the process to a successful conclusion.

Another point to bear in mind is that these are not simple black or white issues. As with most policy issues, there are several options, each attended by pros and cons, which in turn depend on assumptions about which reasonable people can differ. In other words, the Indonesian government is navigating the course toward full budget funding for the TNI without precision instruments. Achieving the goal by 2009 appears to be impossible. Even a five-year timeline would require an improbable combination of good judgment, good discipline, and good luck. Full funding by 2012 or 2015 may be feasible.

Why Is Getting the TNI out of Business and Fully on Budget Important?

A team of Indonesian military experts led by Danang Widoyoko has clearly set forth the rationale for ending the military's business activities.[4] First, the freedom of action the military derives from an independent source of funding weakens the ability of the government to set national goals and determine the means of achieving them. Second, the time and effort absorbed by managing and engaging in business activities diverts individual officers and soldiers from their constitutional duty of defending the nation against external threats and enhancing domestic security.[5] Third, the military's business activities cre-

---

4. Widoyoko and others (2002, pp. 68–69).

5. According to the Constitution of 1945, chap. 12, art. 30, as amended: "(2) The defense and security of the state shall be conducted through the total people's defense and security system, with the Indonesian National Military (TNI) and the Indonesian National Police (POLRI) as the main force, and the people as the supporting force. (3) TNI, consisting of the Army, Navy and Air Force, as an instrument of the state has the duty to defend, protect, and maintain the integrity and sovereignty of the state."

Box 1-1. List of Policy Issues for Getting the TNI out of Business and Fully on Budget

Military Businesses (chapter 6)

Issue 1. What general policy will the government adopt and enforce toward the business activities of government agencies across the board?

Issue 2. How will government policies with respect to military foundations be changed?

Issue 3. How will government policies with respect to military cooperatives be changed?

Issue 4. What policy will the government adopt on the provision of security services by military units?

Issue 5. What policy will the government adopt on the commercialization of state assets owned or controlled by military units?

Issue 6. What policies will the government adopt with regard to military involvement in illegal or criminal income-generating activities?

Issue 7. What approach will the government take to implementing Article 76 of Law No. 34 of 2004?

A National Defense and Security Strategy (chapter 7)

Issues Related to Design

Issue 8. What are the main external threats and what priority should be attached to each one for the purpose of determining the TNI's force structure?

Issue 9. To what extent will Indonesia participate in regional security arrangements?

Issue 10. Will the national defense and security strategy be threat-based or capacity-based?

Issue 11. What will be the respective roles of the TNI and the National Police (Polri) in dealing with threats to public order from domestic terrorists, regional rebellions, and communal violence?

Issue 12. What role will the TNI play in protecting natural and strategic resources?

Issue 13. What role will the TNI play in peacekeeping operations in other countries organized by the United Nations or other international bodies?

Implementation Issues

Issue 14. How will the new TNI doctrine evolve?

Issue 15. What will be the relative strength of the army, navy, and air force?

Issue 16. What will be the role of other forces that can bear some of the burden of internal security?

Issue 17. Will the army's territorial command structure be replaced or modified?

Issue 18. How will intelligence activities be organized, how should official secrets (classified information) be protected, and what information should the public have access to?

Issue 19. Will a new military justice law provide effective disincentives for the TNI to continue engaging in business activities?

The Military Budget (chapter 8)

Major Budget Paramenters

Issue 20. How rapidly will the government allow the military budget to grow over the next five to ten years?

Issue 21. To what extent will regional (*daerah*) governments be permitted to provide financial and other support to the military?

Issue 22. To what extent will the efficiency of the military budget increase?

Issue 23. How much military equipment will be procured from the domestic defense industry?

Issue 24. How much foreign aid will the military be allowed to receive?

Issue 25. How will the government's policy change regarding off-budget financing for the military?

The Welfare of the Soldiers

Issue 26. How will the structure of civil service salaries evolve and will the military salary structure continue to be linked to it?

Issue 27. What provisions will be made for military personnel pensions?

Issue 28. What provisions will be made for military personnel housing benefits?

Issue 29. What provisions will be made for the health and education of military personnel and their families?

Issue 30. What benefits will be made available to disabled soldiers and their widows and orphans?

ate distortions in the nation's economy that lower productivity, misallocate scarce resources, and thereby impede growth. Preferential access to bank credit is an especially corrosive feature of military businesses.

Six months before we began this study, we proposed four sensible principles for managing the military's budget: respect the supremacy of the civilian government in setting priorities and making rules, follow rules rather than operate on a discretionary basis, reinforce transparency and accountability, and strengthen coordination among the government agencies that share responsibility for defense and security (notably the military and the police).[6]

The open debate over national priorities in 1998, in the aftermath of the collapse of the Suharto regime, seemed to suggest that ending the military's role in the economy, "returning the military to the barracks," was high on the country's list. At the beginning of 2007, however, there was scant evidence that transferring to the government the businesses directly or indirectly controlled by the military was one of the top twenty public policy issues.

What Are the Risks of Ending the TNI's Business Activities or of Failing to End Them?

Perhaps the biggest risk in ending the military's business activities is that some officers and soldiers will turn to illegal activities to maintain their current standard of living. This risk can be mitigated by increasing budget-funded TNI salaries and allowances and by gradually phasing out businesses instead of adopting a shock approach. Another risk is that the additional funding required to put the military fully on budget will squeeze out other programs (education, health, infrastructure) that are critical to the country's political stability and economic growth. If allowed to continue its business activities, however, the military might become a destabilizing force in the political life of the country.

Where Are the Data?

Many readers will be frustrated by the small amount of data produced by our study concerning the military's off-budget revenues and expenditures. Unfortunately, reliable data of this nature do not exist in an accessible or reliable form. Although we could have collected anecdotal information and added it up, interpolating to fill in the blanks, we declined to do so because it would inevitably be backward looking and still not produce an accurate picture. We

6. Pramodhawardani in UNSFIR (2005, p. 27).

did, however, devise a "methodology" for estimating the amount of net income generated by the TNI's off-budget activities in 2006 "for operational purposes," which is presented in chapter five.

More important, we have adopted an approach to on-budget and off-budget income and spending that does not depend on data. In any case, the military alone can produce such information, and it shows no indication of being close to doing so. Furthermore, broad political, economic, and cultural forces are combining to steadily shrink the TNI's off-budget income. Therefore we see no advantage in waiting until credible data are available and have instead directed our efforts toward identifying steps that can be taken now to bring Indonesia closer to fully funding its armed forces.

Conclusions

Two main conclusions emerge from our study. First, the amount of money TNI business activities generate "for operational purposes" is much smaller than is commonly believed. Second, it is not feasible to put the TNI fully on the budget by 2009, the deadline set in Law 34 of 2004.

According to conventional wisdom, Indonesia's armed forces have for years obtained 60–70 percent of their funds from a wide range of off-budget business activities and the remainder from the central government's budget. While this estimate may have been accurate at some point in the past, we believe that the net income generated by the TNI's off-budget activities in 2006 and available "for operational purposes" was equivalent to only 1.5–3.0 percent of the government's defense budget for that year. This low estimate results from two critical assumptions:

—Only the net income (profit) of its business activities is "available" to the TNI, not its gross revenues (total sales before expenses).

—Not all of the net income from its business activities is used "for operational purposes."

One assumption has pushed our estimates up: income from off-budget activities is supplemented by income from a few nonbusiness activities, especially "gifts" and "procurement commissions."

An important policy implication of our first main conclusion is that the budget increase required to replace the off-budget funds now flowing to the military is much smaller than is generally assumed. Most emphatically, however, this does not mean that the problem of military businesses has been overblown or should remain on the back burner. On the contrary, we believe that getting the military out of business is essential to accelerating economic growth in Indonesia, consolidating its vibrant but still-fragile democratic system, and achieving a more just and prosperous society.

As already mentioned, 2009 is an unrealistic target for this endeavor. The only way the military could be fully on the budget by then would be to reduce its role in the defense and security of the nation. For example, if it is assumed that Indonesia faces no "conventional" external threats that would have to be repulsed by conventional military units (infantry and artillery battalions, submarines and destroyers, fighter squadrons, and so on), then the budget required to maintain the current number of military personnel at their current level of operational readiness may not be much larger than its present level. Or if it is assumed that all internal threats related to secessionist movements, communal violence, terrorism, and the like will be addressed by the National Police, then the current budget may be adequate.

Few military experts, government officials, politicians, or segments of the voting population would subscribe to such a modest role for the TNI. Realistically, serious options range from a "minimal essential force" that may be achievable in the medium term to a somewhat more robust force. An "ideal" force, on a par with that of Malaysia or Thailand, for example, appears to be out of the question in the next ten to fifteen years.

Given the extremely low operational readiness of today's TNI, not to mention the obstacles to efficient planning, budgeting, and procurement, it appears impossible to raise the operational readiness of the TNI's existing forces to the 80–90 percent level by 2009. It may be possible to do so by 2012. Equipping and training a restructured TNI to be more effective in supporting the defense and security objectives of the democratically elected government may also be feasible by 2012 but would presumably be more costly.

Four large obstacles stand in the way of putting the TNI fully on the budget by 2009. First, the military culture, which is more in the spirit of the Suharto era than the Reformasi (Reformation) era, reinforces business activities. Pecuniary incentives also play a powerful role in maintaining these activities. Second, the military lacks a credible strategic plan or framework and thus is loath to move away from its business orientation to a more professional one. Third, as long as the country's economic growth rate is stuck in the range of 5–6 percent a year, the central government will be on a tight budget. Fourth, the democratic system introduced in stages after Suharto's resignation has been giving high priority to education and other social sectors over defense and security.

Some further conclusions relate specifically to the TNI's business activities.

—The main benefit of the military's business activities is employment, not only for military personnel but also for their family members and friends. These activities are akin to a public sector employment program, and there is no reason to believe that the TNI is a more efficient employer than other public sector agencies.

—Military businesses are expenditure-maximizing rather than profit-maximizing entities; as such, they make important contributions to the welfare of military personnel who might otherwise engage in more harmful behavior.

—Almost all public sector bodies have created "foundations" that function as holding companies for various business activities. Instead of being instruments to promote social welfare, they function as money-laundering mechanisms in a way that is impossible to reconcile with good governance. Although it may be possible to improve the transparency and accountability of the military's foundations, closing them down or separating them meaningfully from individual commands will be resisted as long as other foundations in the public sector are allowed to do business as usual. Even if the process of dissolving TNI foundations begins immediately, it will take some time because settling the claims of nonmilitary shareholders and creditors will be difficult and time-consuming. Nonetheless, the TNI could set an example by leading the Indonesian government out of this wilderness.

—Cooperatives constitute another subsector of military businesses. Most of them are small, serve useful social purposes, are more transparent than the foundations, and are more accountable to their members. Closing them down would probably incur heavy costs in morale that would outweigh any economic efficiency and military professionalism gained by doing so. As for the few cooperatives that have grown into substantial business conglomerates, any abuses there could be greatly reduced by separating them from their host commands, putting them into the hands of experienced civilian managers, and increasing the transparency of their operations.

—Putting on budget the revenue from commercialization of state assets is another particularly attractive area of reform. Currently little if any of this revenue appears to be reflected in the central government's budget, despite various budget laws and regulations requiring that it be included. Since almost all other ministries and agencies generate off-budget revenue from the commercialization of state assets, it may be difficult to put the military's revenues from this source on the budget until comparable discipline is applied to the rest of the government.

—A strong case also exists for putting on budget the income generated by the military's security services, such as those provided for Freeport-McMoRan Copper & Gold in Papua until early 2006.

—For better or worse, Article 76 of Law 34/2004 has created a benchmark for progress in this area of military reform. With its credibility at stake in the elections of 2009, the SBY government is running out of time to resolve the issues that have delayed the implementing regulation called for in Article 76 and visibly begin transferring individual business units to the government, privatizing them, or closing them down.

The pace of progress in getting the TNI out of business will be heavily influenced by the evolution of the defense budget. The size and composition of the defense budget will in turn depend on many factors.

—The government is in the process of reforming the civil service, particularly restructuring the compensation system to make it less discretionary and more closely linked to performance. Reform of the TNI's compensation system could lead or lag behind this effort, but probably not by very much.

—It is unrealistic to expect the national defense and security strategy scheduled to be issued in the first half of 2007 to be fully credible. A half-credible strategy could provide a sufficient basis for making sensible choices with respect to many of the issues we have highlighted in our study.

—The territorial command structure of the army will be a major obstacle to reducing the TNI's access to off-budget income. Generating off-budget income is deeply rooted in the daily activities of the personnel in the territorial commands. It may not be possible to bring the military establishment up to a professional level until the territorial command structure is modified or replaced with a structure more clearly linked to defending the nation against critical external and internal threats.

—Studies commissioned by the Ministry of Defense could lay the groundwork for more effective use of budget resources for improving the welfare of soldiers, especially in the areas of health care, education, and the support of crippled soldiers, widows, and orphans.

—Well-targeted technical and financial assistance from foreign countries and international institutions could help move the TNI out of business and on the budget at a faster pace.

The Flow of the Study

Our analysis opens in chapter 2 with a word about the global and domestic contexts of TNI financing. Several developments at the international level merit attention: recent geopolitical changes, which have reduced the need for a military structure designed to defend against conventional attacks; the unlicensed exploitation of Indonesia's forest and marine resources, which is its greatest external threat today; the growth of regional cooperation in Southeast Asia; the global trend in strengthening civilian control over the military; and technological advancements. Another important consideration is the scope for foreign assistance in enhancing the military's operational capacity and professional character.

On the domestic front, the business activities of the military are part of a decades-old cultural pattern that has become deeply embedded in almost every corner of government. It is unrealistic—especially in view of the fragility of Indonesia's eight-year-old democracy—to expect the military to alter this pattern as long as it remains strong in the rest of the public sector, and indeed in the private sector as well. To complicate matters, there is an uneasy and unstable division of responsibilities between the military and police for containing terrorism, separatism, and ethnic/communal unrest. In addition, constraints on the budget itself have historically provided the basic rationale for the military's engagement in an immense range of business activities.

The main body of the book is divided into two parts focusing on the twin goals of getting the TNI out of business and fully funding a professional TNI from the central government budget. As pointed out in chapter 3, reform cannot be attempted without an understanding of the history of military business since independence, which evolved in four stages (for a brief account of the history and structure of the military itself, see appendix A). During the struggle for independence (1945–50), localized income-generating activities by the disparate units fighting the Dutch became critical to their operational effectiveness. In the Sukarno era (1950–65), the military's role in the economy expanded sharply when most foreign-owned businesses were nationalized and military officers were assigned to manage many of them. As a share of domestic output, the value added by these business activities probably peaked in the middle of the Suharto era (1965–98) and then began a slow decline, squeezed out by the growing business ambitions of Suharto's family and friends. A subsequent blow was the financial crisis of 1997–98, which destroyed the banking system, wiped out many "modern" (military and non-military) businesses dependent on access to large amounts of credit, and gave birth to the Reformasi era (1998–). Antimilitary sentiment since then has contributed to further erosion of TNI businesses.

The military's business activities in all spheres—formal, informal, and legal—are laid out in chapter 4, and our "methodology" for estimating the size of the TNI's off-budget income in 2006 follows in chapter five. The calculations behind these estimates appear in appendix B.

Chapter 6 examines the process of implementing Article 76 of Law 34/2004, which requires that all of the military's business activities be transferred to the government by 2009. The challenge of meeting the Article 76 deadline falls squarely on the shoulders of President SBY, who may be running for reelection in 2009. This chapter also raises seven of the thirty policy issues highlighted in our study.

Turning to the goal of full funding, chapter 7 notes the current policy vacuum and the need for at least some elements of a credible national defense and security strategy before the budget amounts for full funding of the TNI can be determined. The discussion then focuses on six policy issues related to designing such a strategy and another six related to its implementation.

Chapter 8 takes up the current military budget, projected out to 2012 for three scenarios: base case, low growth, and high growth. Six of the relevant policy issues here relate to major budget parameters and five to the welfare of the soldiers.

Reluctant to prescribe specific policy measures because of the nature of our study, we nevertheless have been persuaded to offer a few general observations and highlight some implications. We do this in chapter 9, the last part of the book.

2

Policy Context:
External and Internal Factors

Indonesia's decision to end the off-budget business activities of Tentara Nasional Indonesia (TNI) and put the military entirely on the budget by 2009 is a vital yet ambitious one, considering the dynamic context in which it must be implemented. At least six external factors and six internal factors will have a bearing on the outcome.

External Factors

Three of the external factors have to do with geopolitical developments: the end of the cold war, the growth of regional cooperation, and the intensification of nonmilitary threats. Three others relate more narrowly to military matters: the experience of other countries in establishing civilian control over the military, the impact of technology on military equipment requirements, and the availability of military assistance.

The Post–Cold War World

The exceptional stability and economic growth Indonesia experienced under the thirty-year rule of President Suharto were closely linked to the cold war. He consolidated power amid a bloody cataclysm in 1965–66, during which hundreds of thousands of Communist Party members and suspected sympathizers were massacred by pro-West elements of the military and other social groups.[1] Suharto quickly moved his country toward the Western camp, severing political and military ties with the Soviet bloc and China. Subse-

1. Friend (2003, pp. 100–25).

quently, billions of dollars in aid were obtained from the United States and its cold war partners.

With the collapse of the Soviet Union, the cold war rationale for supporting Suharto's regime evaporated. In the face of escalating cronyism, corruption, and human rights abuses by the military, Western donors began cutting back aid to Indonesia. Domestic opponents of the Suharto regime took comfort in the knowledge that the donor countries were likely to welcome a new government.[2]

After 1991, as the triumphant democracies of the West became less tolerant of right-wing, often military-based, autocratic regimes, external support for the TNI also eroded quickly. In addition, the TNI was blamed for permitting, if not instigating, a massacre of pro-independence supporters in the former Portuguese colony of East Timor in November 1991.[3] Serious human rights abuses linked to the TNI also occurred after Suharto resigned: again in East Timor following a referendum on independence in 1999, in Maluku Province in connection with religious conflicts that broke out in 1999, and in Aceh Province during a heavy-handed campaign against the secessionist movement.[4]

After the terrorist attacks on the World Trade Center towers and the Pentagon on September 11, 2001, however, the tide of negative external opinion toward the TNI began to turn. A year later, Indonesia became a front-line state in the war against international terrorism when a gruesome suicide bombing occurred on Bali. It was followed by attacks on the J. W. Marriott Hotel in Jakarta in August 2003 and the Australian embassy in Jakarta in September 2004. A second bombing occurred on Bali in October 2005. As the world's most populous Muslim-majority nation, Indonesia is now being wooed by the United States and other countries leading the fight against global terrorism. The TNI is seen as an important ally in this fight.[5]

Other geopolitical trends have mixed implications for the TNI. For most of Indonesia's history as an independent nation, military forces around the world were organized and equipped primarily to defend their countries against external attacks. Since Iraq's invasion of Kuwait in 1991, however, there have been no cross-border wars and the defense and security strategies of many countries have been adjusted to downplay direct military attacks by

2. Schwarz (1994, p. 304).

3. Indonesia took possession of East Timor by military force in 1975, after Portugal cut it loose along with its other overseas colonies. The western half of the island was the part of the Netherlands East Indies that became Indonesia when independence was declared in 1945.

4. O'Rourke (2002, pp. 155–56, 164–65, 234–35).

5. Wise (2005, pp. 67–78).

unfriendly countries.[6] Furthermore, the military capacity of most countries, as measured by the share of military spending in gross domestic product (GDP), has been declining.

Though cross-border military aggression has declined around the world, ethnic and communal violence within countries has increased. Indonesia has not been immune from this pattern. It has faced a succession of internal security challenges from its earliest days as an independent nation. For the past fifty years, the TNI's primary operational task has been to maintain the country's territorial integrity and is likely to remain so for the foreseeable future.

Regional Cooperation

Over the past ten to twenty years, the power equation in Asia has become increasingly complex. Historic rivalries among Japan, China, and India stand in the way of the kind of broad regional cooperation, as achieved in Europe. The ten members of the Association of Southeast Asian Nations (ASEAN) in the shadow of these three Asian powers have much to gain from strengthening regional cooperation, but even economic integration has proceeded at a snail's pace owing to strong nationalist sentiments in most ASEAN countries.

The United States is also a vital element of the power equation in Asia. To assert its leadership in the broad Asia-Pacific region, the United States created Asia-Pacific Economic Cooperation (APEC) in 1989, which holds annual summit meetings. In 1993 the ASEAN countries created the ASEAN Regional Forum (ARF), with many of the same members as APEC, to pursue an Asian-centered cooperation agenda.[7]

Indonesia is the natural leader of the Southeast Asian nations because of its size and its formally nonaligned position in global politics. In the turmoil following the fall of the Suharto regime, it assumed a lower profile in ASEAN, APEC, and other regional activities. However, the strong electoral mandate obtained by President Susilo Bambang Yudhoyono (SBY) in 2004 has allowed Indonesia to reassert its leadership role.

6. British military strategist Rupert Smith argues that "war no longer exists" and that the principal military challenge in the future will be "continuous criss-crossing between confrontation and conflict, whilst peace is not necessarily either the starting or the end point" (2005, pp. 1, 16–17).

7. The objectives of the ARF are "(1) to foster constructive dialogue and consultation on political and security issues of common interest and concern; and (2) to make significant contributions to efforts towards confidence-building and preventive diplomacy in the Asia-Pacific region." ARF meetings are held once a year at the foreign minister level in conjunction with ASEAN's Post–Ministerial Conference.

With the exception of security provided for the Malaka Strait, military cooperation in Southeast Asia remains in its infancy.[8] The tendency within ASEAN has been to emphasize economic cooperation over other forms of cooperation. In recent years, however, interest in developing regional security arrangements has begun to take tangible form.

Based on the "ASEAN Vision 2020" adopted in 1997, the ASEAN Security Community became one of the three pillars of the ASEAN Community, along with the ASEAN Economic Community and the ASEAN Sociocultural Community. A key step in developing the ASEAN Security Community was the initiation in May 2006 of an annual ASEAN defense ministers' meeting (ADMM) following years of careful preparation, which included meetings of ASEAN chiefs of defense forces, as well as army, navy, and air force chiefs. A legally binding Convention on Counter Terrorism was signed at the ASEAN Summit in January 2007.

In the early years of Reformasi, piracy in the Malaka Strait reached an alarming level and provided a strong impetus for cooperation among Singapore, Malaysia, and Thailand.[9] As a result of their efforts, the Lloyds shipping insurance syndicate was able to de-list the strait as a war zone in August 2006 and to lower premiums for ships passing through it.

Nonmilitary Threats

Arguably the greatest threat Indonesia faces today is the unlicensed exploitation of its exceptionally diverse and enormously valuable marine and tropical forest resources.[10] It has never had effective control of its borders. Foreigners enter with little risk to poach fish and illegally cut timber, which are smuggled out of the country in large quantities.

Indonesia is reportedly losing $8 billion worth of stolen fish to foreigners every year.[11] The illegal extraction of timber is taking place at the rate of 40 million cubic meters a year (although the amount of illegally exported tim-

8. Indonesia signed a landmark agreement on security cooperation with Australia in November 2006.

9. The Malaka Strait is 550 miles long and 330 miles wide at the north end, funneling down to 1.5 miles at its narrowest point. Forty percent of world trade passes through this strait, including 80 percent of Chinese oil imports; 80 percent of Japanese, Taiwanese, and South Korean oil and gas imports; and two-thirds of the world's liquefied natural gas. Roughly 600 freighters pass through every day. Singapore, at the south end of the strait, is the world's largest port. Percival (2005, pp. 1, 4, 22–25).

10. Indonesia's territory includes 17,500 islands. Percival (2005, p. 25). Its archipelagic waters extend over 6 million square kilometers. Sebastian (2006, p. 240).

11. Percival (2005, p. 33). Widjajanto and Prasetyono (2006, p. 4) put the loss at $3 billion to $4 billion a year.

ber and timber products appears to have fallen from 10 million cubic meters a year to less than 3 million cubic meters, this lower amount still represents a retail value on the order of $6 billion).[12] And Indonesia's loss from smuggled gasoline and other heavily subsidized refined products apparently reached upward of $850 million in 2005.[13]

The TNI, the Marine Police, and seven other agencies of the central government share responsibilities for countering these threats, but their technical capacity to do so is minimal.[14] Furthermore, they are widely believed to be part of the problem.[15]

Global Experience with Civilian Control

Indonesia is far from being unique in having a military establishment heavily engaged in off-budget economic activities. Every region of the world has seen variations on this theme. Even "modern" armies like that of the United Kingdom have, in the not-too-distant past, generated resources for operational purposes from business activities beyond the production of military equipment and services (defense industries).[16] The U.S. military, with a long history as a purely professional establishment, is more the exception than the rule.

Still, the current trend toward civilian control is clear, even in nondemocratic countries like China. Equally clear is the difficulty Indonesia will face in achieving a high standard of good governance as long as the military has independent sources of financing. Furthermore, the degree of respect the TNI commands beyond the borders of Indonesia will depend in large part on how quickly it extracts itself from business activities and concentrates on military missions.

Technological Change

Although military technology has been evolving rapidly since the end of the cold war, the TNI still relies on obsolete weapons and support systems. Most

12. Obidzinski, Andrianto, and Wijaya (2006, pp. 25–26).

13. Donald Greenlees, "Asia Oil Subsidies Bring Windfall to Smugglers," *International Herald Tribune,* September 27, 2005.

14. The other agencies come under the Ministry of Transportation (Sea and Coast Guard Unit, National Search and Rescue Agency), the Ministry of Marine Affairs and Fisheries (Surveillance and Control of Marine and Fish Resources), the Ministry of Finance (customs), and the Ministry of Justice and Human Rights (immigration). In addition, the decentralization of 2001 enhanced the authority of regional entities that have coastlines. The National Police claims primary law enforcement responsibility in territorial waters to a distance of 12 nautical miles from the coast. Percival (2005, pp. 28, 30).

15. Percival (2005, p. 8).

16. According to a study of the military's business activities in Myanmar/Burma, it "followed the British Army's style of running services for its troops." Nurhasim (2005, p. 191).

new technologies are expensive in terms of procurement, training, and maintenance, but not all. Satellite imagery and unmanned drones, for example, can provide more information at a lower cost than manned surveillance aircraft.

Finding a cost-effective mix of technologies will be a major challenge for the Ministry of Defense and the TNI. Success will greatly depend on whether and how soon the three military services can be shaped into a structure that is durable and not reoriented every few years.

Availability of Military Assistance

During its independence struggle, Indonesia relied on American military equipment and training. Then in the Sukarno era it obtained generous naval and air support from the Soviet Union and China, although the army maintained close ties with the United States. Under Suharto, equipment purchases from the Soviet bloc ceased, and the United States became the dominant supplier of both equipment and training.[17] U.S. support in this period was instrumental in creating a cadre of U.S.-trained and reform-minded officers, typified by President SBY.[18]

After the beginning of Reformasi in 1998, military assistance remained small, in large part because the government was unable to establish accountability for human rights violations in the past.[19] In 2005, however, the U.S. Congress removed its ban on military training and its embargo on the sale of lethal military equipment imposed after the rampage in East Timor in 1999. Given the intense U.S. interest in supporting Indonesia as a Muslim democracy and because of its strategic role in Southeast Asia, the potential for a substantial increase in U.S. training and equipment sales is clear.[20]

---

17. Between 1965 and 2005, more than 4,000 TNI personnel attended courses under the U.S. International Military Education and Training (IMET) Program. Haseman (2006, p. 120). Between 1975 and 1999, the U.S. government approved more than $1 billion in arms sales to Indonesia. Jamaluddin (2006, p. 21).

18. President SBY attended Airborne and Ranger courses at Fort Benning, Georgia, in 1976; the Infantry Officer Advance Course at Fort Benning in 1982–83; and the U.S. Army's Command and General Staff College in Fort Leavenworth in 1990–91.

19. The apparent impunity of the TNI's intelligence establishment was highlighted by the poisoning of Indonesian human rights leader Munir Sahid Talib on a Garuda Airlines flight to Amsterdam in September 2004. An airline pilot was convicted of the murder and sentenced to fourteen years in prison, presumably acting on the orders of a powerful military or intelligence figure. But the Supreme Court overruled the sentence in October 2006, making the pilot eligible for release after less than three years. The source of his orders was never established.

20. See Lachica and others (2004); and Haseman and Lachica (2005).

Offers of military assistance have already poured in from the European Union members, Australia, Japan, China, India, Russia, and other suppliers. The terms of this assistance are becoming more favorable as competition intensifies, but the Indonesian government has yet to demonstrate a capacity to make sensible trade-offs between quality and financing.

Internal Factors

Six internal factors will have an impact on the government's goal of putting the TNI fully on budget by 2009: deeply rooted cultural patterns, the fragility of the new political system, institutional weaknesses, endemic public sector corruption, the challenges of domestic security, and budget constraints.

The Cultural Quicksand

The Constitution of 1945 envisioned Indonesia as an "independent, united, sovereign, just, and prosperous" nation. One great difficulty in realizing this vision is that Indonesia, like all countries, is a prisoner of its history and culture, despite its remarkable transition from autocratic to democratic rule in 1998. This legacy accounts for the population's fierce resistance to many promising reforms proposed by the government. Indonesia seems mired in quicksand. It lags behind other Asian countries, notably China and India, even though it was once in the company of Korea, Malyasia, and other Asian economic "tigers" in the 1980s and early 1990s.

The paramount cultural reality of Indonesia is a small, densely populated island (Java), holding roughly 60 percent of the population, at the center of an archipelago characterized by immense ethnic and religious diversity. It is almost a miracle that Indonesia has not fragmented into a multitude of mini-states. What binds it together is not so much a shared vision of the future but the struggle for independence from colonial rule, the independence movement's inspired decision to adopt Bahasa Indonesia (a second language for everyone) as the national language, and Suharto's felicitous decision to support the economic policies advocated by a small group of U.S.-trained technocrats as he was consolidating power in the late 1960s.

The underlying cultural tensions are reflected in two contradictory trends, toward regionalism, on one hand, and nationalism, on the other. Regional autonomy has been strengthened enormously through the exceptional decentralization of administrative authority implemented at the beginning of 2001, and through the Special Autonomy status granted to Aceh at the western end of the archipelago and Papua at the eastern end. At the same time, nationalism is rampant. The government's public commitment to a unitary state—Negara Kesatuan Republik Indonesia (NKRI)—has become a sacred obligation, with the TNI being both the leading apostle of NKRI and its enforcer. One manifestation of this nationalism is the country's skeptical attitude toward foreign investment.

To add to the country's social confusion, the deeply rooted and "involuted" culture of the Javanese heartland retains a feudal character from beyond the fifteenth century, when most regional rulers adopted Islam. Patronage remains the primary instrument of power. Personalities are more important than institutions, a pattern illustrated by the phrase *asal bapak senang* (as long as the boss is happy), abbreviated as ABS.

These circumstances make it difficult to arrive at a social consensus on most issues and thus have enabled the TNI to become a state within the state. Only the TNI's own clear vision of Indonesia as a unitary state, many citizens believe, keeps the country together and moving toward a just and prosperous society.

The Fragile Democratic System

The path toward democratic governance since 1998 has been far from smooth. The nineteen-month term of President Habibie was dominated by the economic damage of the 1997 financial crisis and the traumatic loss of East Timor. The indirect election of President Wahid in 1999 was a giant step toward a democratic regime, but his idiosyncratic leadership became increasingly dysfunctional, and he was forced from office less than halfway through his five-year term. President Megawati brought political stability to the country but not sufficient economic progress or leadership skill to win the country's first direct presidential election in 2004, which put SBY into office. Despite SBY's resounding electoral victory and considerable popularity, Indonesia's democracy remains fragile and is not yet meeting citizens' aspirations in the areas of prosperity and fairness.

The feeling of prosperity in the decade leading up to the financial crisis of 1997 was so great that many Indonesians are nostalgic about that period, despite the abuses of power that ultimately brought the Suharto regime down. In the year following the crisis, the country's GDP fell by more than 13 percent. Although the subsequent recovery was steady, with GDP growing at 5–6 percent a year, the pace now seems stuck below the 7–8 percent sustained during the Suharto era. It is hard for a young democracy to thrive in a low-growth environment.

To a significant degree, the economy's uninspiring performance is a product of Indonesia's immature democratic system:

—While the government appears to understand the reforms needed to raise foreign and domestic investment to the level required to support rapid growth, it lacks the political power to push through essential legislation or to implement it effectively when it is passed.

—The regime's weak support in the House of Representatives (Dewan Perwakilan Rakyat, DPR) is due in large part to the number of parties that won seats, the ease of creating new parties, and the nature of the parties. Although the number of parties in the DPR shrank from forty-eight in 1999 to twenty-four in 2004 and would drop even further under a new law being debated, the political system is fluid and undeveloped. Three of the largest parties (Golkar, PDI-P, and PKB) are divided internally and may not fully resolve these differences before the 2009 election.

—Only two political parties, Golkar and PDI-P, are competitive across the country. The others tend to draw their strength from particular regions. Most of the parties are dominated by individuals who maintain their leadership positions by distributing party funds that come overwhelmingly from the business community, not from voters attracted by party platforms.

Institutional Weaknesses

In recent years development experts have come to recognize that institutions—especially administrative and judicial institutions that support the "rule of law"—play an important role in achieving sustainable economic growth. By all accounts, institutional weakness is one of Indonesia's biggest handicaps. Laws are passed and regulations are issued, but implementation lags seriously behind. Far from fostering the kind of legal certainty that attracts foreign or domestic investment, the judicial system, a tool of the government under the Suharto regime, has been a major disappointment in the Reformasi era.

One of Reformasi's signal achievements, the decentralization launched in 2001, proved to be another source of institutional weakness. Authority passed from the central government to the country's districts (*kabupaten*) and municipalities (*kota madya*), bypassing the provinces, yet institutions at this level were far weaker than the already shaky ones at the center.[21] While decentralization seems to have been successful from a political perspective, the economic impact may have been negative as regional authorities introduced new taxes and other barriers to commerce and gave high priority to using their allocated share of the central government's revenue to boost the salaries and perks of regional legislators and officials.

21. Indonesia's 31 provinces plus the Special Capital Region of Jakarta and the Special Region of Yogyakarta are currently divided into 349 districts and 90 municipalities.

Endemic Corruption

TNI personnel have been engaging in off-budget revenue-generating activities for more than five decades, much as their more numerous counterparts in the civilian bureaucracy have done.[22] It is hard to find any ministry or government agency that does not generate off-budget revenue from a wide range of commercial and rent-seeking activities.[23]

Many external observers would call the system corrupt, whereas internal observers would say corruption is the system. In other words, corruption (as defined by the democratic West) is not exceptional behavior in Indonesian society today; it is normal behavior.

Proposals for military reform that fail to take this pervasive attitude into account are unlikely to succeed. It is unrealistic, for example, to expect TNI officers to support families on official salaries alone when other government employees are enjoying incomes that are multiples of their official salaries.

The problem is reflected in the characterization of bureaucratic positions and military commands as "wet" (*basah*, meaning they provide good access to off-budget revenue) or "dry" (*kering*)—a distinction that goes back to the early colonial period, predating independence by more than a century. It is also reflected in the practice of paying to join the civil service or the military, or paying to be promoted to lucrative positions.[24]

During the Suharto era, organizations such as Transparency International ranked Indonesia among the most corrupt countries in the world. Its relative performance continues to be poor. Altough the SBY government, more than any other since independence, is openly tackling the problem of corruption and taking steps to diminish it, this will be a long uphill battle. It may take a generation or more to move Indonesia from its position as one of the most corrupt countries in the world to the middle of the pack or better.

The latest report on corruption, copublished by the United States–Indonesia Society and the Centre for Strategic and International Studies,

22. "It is difficult to overstate the seriousness of the problem of corruption in Indonesia. Corruption is pervasive—that is, almost no sector of society is free of corruption. It is deeply embedded in the fabric of society and institutions. . . . Rather than being an aberration, corruption has been a core norm of Indonesia's political economy for decades." Davidsen, Juwono, and Timberman (2006, p. 9).

23. "The sociologist W. F. Wertheim has suggested that it was only after the creation of the Napoleonic state in Europe that officials were expected to keep their private business separate from their public activities." Crouch (1975–76, pp. 538–39).

24. For example, the payment required to become an ordinary army soldier posted in Jakarta was reportedly Rp 30 million to 40 million ($3,000–$4,000). The corresponding payment to join the National Police was Rp 50 million ($5,500). Interview with taxi driver in Jakarta, June 2006.

notes that "only limited action [has been] taken against those at the apex of power in Indonesia, namely politicians and generals who currently hold high level positions in the national government, political parties or military." Although the report deals primarily with the civil service, it calls attention to the corruption related to military procurement and the operation of the TNI's foundations, cooperatives, and businesses.[25]

The Challenges of Domestic Security

One of the most important achievements of the Reformasi era was the separation of the National Police (Polri) from the armed forces in 1999.[26] Even so, four distinct domestic threats are beyond the capacity of the police at the present time and are likely to require TNI attention over the medium term at least: secessionist movements, communal violence, terrorism, and natural disasters.

Assuming the 2005 peace accord for Aceh continues to be implemented successfully, the only serious secessionist threat remaining is centered in Papua, the Indonesian half of the island of New Guinea. The native inhabitants of this resource-rich, thinly populated territory are aboriginals who are ethnically distinct from the vast majority of Indonesians. Most native Papuans live in the mountainous interior with limited access to the modern world. Missionaries have converted many of them to Christianity. After Indonesia gained control of Papua in 1963 under a questionable UN-mandated plebiscite, non-Papuan Indonesians began to settle on the coast in large numbers and to exploit Papua's rich mineral and timber resources. In 2001, to address grievances that had built up over four decades, the Indonesian House of Representatives passed a law granting Papua Special Autonomy. Poor implementation of this law, however, has created new grievances.

Indonesia's "resource curse" is most evident in Papua. The revenue currently generated by the Freeport-McMoRan mining operation alone exceeds the amount needed to meet the needs of the current residents. A new and large stream of revenue will soon begin flowing from BP's natural gas project at Tangguh. Logging revenues are also high, although extremely difficult to estimate because most are linked to illegal extraction.

Over the past couple of years, the TNI has increased the number of units assigned to Papua. The trend is worrisome because many Papuan natives view

25. Davidsen and others (2006, pp. 2, 43–45).

26. The National Police falls outside the scope of our study. However, the business activities of the National Police are substantial and in some respects even more problematical. Numerous people interviewed remarked, for example, that corruption in the National Police is much worse than corruption in the TNI.

the TNI more as a threat to their security than as a guardian. Beefing up the TNI presence in Papua may conceivably fuel secessionist sentiment rather than quell it, yet the National Police do not have the capacity to maintain law and order there. Hence the potential for economic criminals and political opportunists to foster serious disorder is undeniable and cannot be exaggerated. Furthermore, after the loss of East Timor, public sentiment in the rest of the country is strongly in favor of crushing the separatist movement in Papua.

Since independence, communal violence has erupted periodically in many parts of the archipelago aside from Papua and Aceh. The most serious conflicts in the Reformasi era have occurred in the islands of Maluku (between Christians and Muslims), in Central Sulawesi (between Christians and Muslims), and in Kalimantan (mostly between Christian Dayak natives and immigrants from other islands). It is difficult to predict the level of communal violence in the future. To the extent that it is driven by economic hardship, steady growth or more rapid growth may militate against more incidents.

Since separating from the TNI, the police have earned high marks for their pursuit of terrorists within Indonesia, especially in connection with the bombing of two nightclubs in Bali in October 2002. Nevertheless, the multiple terrorist attacks in Indonesia combined with the war on global terrorism led by the United States have kept the TNI in the game and will undoubtedly keep it involved for some time.

The tsunami that struck Aceh and Nias at the end of 2004 highlighted not only the constructive role the TNI can play in responding to natural disasters but also its weaknesses in this regard. Even so, the TNI could be assigned a greater role in disaster relief, especially since Indonesia is more vulnerable to natural disasters than most countries, being situated on one of the most geologically active spots on the planet. The benefits of an effective TNI response are also large in terms of public support in a democratic system for a well-equipped, well-trained, and well-compensated military force, while the costs of equipping and training military units for disaster relief and reconstruction are relatively low. Furthermore, this equipment and training would be closely related to other domestic missions, such as curbing communal violence, or combating the problem of haze related to illegal land clearing in Sumatra and Kalimantan. It is also relevant to participation in UN peace-building missions in other countries.[27]

27. According to an *Antara* news report on August 16, 2006, Commander Air Marshal Djoko Suyanto of the TNI announced the formation of a rapid response force to handle natural disasters. The force would number 3,426 personnel from the army, marines, air force, and civilian specialists.

Budget Constraints

For 2007, the military share of the central government budget is Rp 32.6 trillion ($3.4 billion at the assumed exchange rate of U.S.$1 = Rp 9,300), or 6.3 percent of the central government budget, which is equivalent to 0.9 percent of GDP. This represents a 16 percent increase over the military budget in 2006 (unadjusted for inflation). The TNI's budget has been growing more rapidly in the Reformasi era than most other components of the budget, but the GDP share remains low by regional and global standards.[28]

Indonesia's total public sector revenue in relation to GDP is on the low side, but pushing the share up to the emerging market average is not feasible in the short run. The good news here is that a number of the Ministry of Revenue's ambitious reforms regarding tax collection seem to be boosting tax revenue.

Another basic political reality is that defense and security have not been a top budget priority since the campaign to gain control of Papua in the 1950s. Budget priorities in the Reformasi era continue to favor other sectors, especially education. Under the Constitution of 1945 (Article 31), at least 20 percent of the central and regional government budgets is to be allocated to education.[29] Consequently the scope for increasing the military budget will be quite limited between now and 2009—and probably will remain so for at least the next ten years.

28. It should also be kept in mind that the cost of equivalent defense and security in an archipelagic nation will be higher than for a continental nation of similar population size and land area.

29. In 2006, roughly 9 percent of the budget was allocated to education.

PART I

*Getting Out of Business
and Ending Off-Budget Funding*

3

The Legacies of Sukarno and Suharto and the Shock of Reformasi

As mentioned earlier, the military's business activities began from the moment independence was declared in 1945, expanded steadily during the Sukarno era, reached their apex in the 1980s under President Suharto, and then unraveled in the financial crisis of 1997, which also triggered the collapse of the Suharto regime. They were further weakened by developments during Reformasi, most notably the passage of the TNI Law of 2004, which set a deadline of 2009 for the TNI to fully divest its business activities and rely solely on funding from the central government.

The Fight for Independence (1945–49)

In the nation's struggle for independence during 1945–49, "regular" soldiers and irregular militias—the embryo of the Indonesian Armed Forces (Angkatan Bersenjata Republik Indonesia, ABRI)—were desperate for money to fund their operations.[1] The only way to pay and equip soldiers in the fight to end colonial rule was through a variety of business activities. These experiences provided models for the structure and justification of many such activities even today.

Each Indonesian combat unit had to find its own sources of support. Smuggling (rubber, copra) and drug trafficking (opium) were among the most profitable and common sources.[2] Activities of this kind were hardly

1. For more details, see appendix A. The title *ABRI* was adopted early in the Suharto era and encompassed the army, navy, air force, and police. When the National Police was separated from ABRI in 1999, the military forces became the Tentara Nasional Indonesia (TNI).

2. Another precedent was the self-defense force created by the Japanese during their occupation of Indonesia, which was largely self-financed. Basri (2001, p. 279).

unique to Indonesia. Revolutionary and other nonconventional, non-state forces have generated revenue from "illegal" activities from time immemorial and are still doing so in most regions of the world. This self-financing had a considerable impact: it fostered a sense of economic independence from the government, distanced the TNI from the corrupt practices of civilian politicians, and reinforced ABRI's self-image as the principal guardian of the nation's sovereignty and revolutionary spirit.

The Sukarno Era (1950–65)

The independence struggle ended in 1950, when the Netherlands government and the revolutionary government of Indonesia, led by Sukarno, negotiated a transfer of power based on a new constitution giving the country a parliamentary form of government and a federal structure. Neither of these features endured. Successive governments were short-lived as parties with widely divergent visions competed for power. Policies were inconsistent or unclear, the economy stagnated, and regional tensions grew. However, serious secessionist movements were prevented from achieving their goals by a series of ABRI operations.

Indonesia's experiment with parliamentary government ended in 1957 when Sukarno declared martial law. Two years later he restored the 1945 Constitution by decree and nationalized foreign companies. Soon distortions in the economy became severe, and an ideological civil war between procommunist and anticommunist forces began to dominate the political landscape. These unsustainable trends were resolved after an attempted coup in 1965 linked to the Communist Party was stopped by army units led by General Suharto. A year-long orgy of bloody recriminations wiped out the communists as well as many uninvolved citizens, but it took Suharto another three years to consolidate power and engineer his succession to the presidency.

The military organization that emerged victorious from the independence struggle developed a doctrine that gave it a central role in the country's political life. The doctrine was rooted in a strategy of guerrilla-style resistance ("people's warfare") against external attacks. In support of the strategy, the country was divided into "territorial army commands" at the provincial, residency, district, and subdistrict level. In addition, noncommissioned officers (NCOs) were posted to individual villages. Commanders at each level were responsible for generating off-budget revenue to supplement the meager funding provided by the central government budget. In 1958 General A. H. Nasution, the dominant military figure of the era, expanded on the original doctrine by providing a rationale for allowing active and retired military officers to occupy key positions in the civilian government, state-owned enterprises, and private companies. The new doctrine became known as *dwifungsi* (dual function).[3]

ABRI's role in the economy expanded sharply when at the end of 1957 the government nationalized Dutch companies and put military officers in charge of many of them. Military business received another boost during this period when the civilian government was unable to raise enough revenue from the economy to fully fund the defense budget required to support the defense and security mission assigned to ABRI.

Three important forms of military business emerged in the Sukarno era: partnerships, cooperatives, and foundations. Partnerships were established between military commanders and successful businessmen, often from the Indonesian-Chinese community. Cooperatives were organized by individual commands at all levels to ensure the supply of basic goods to soldiers and their families. Foundations (*yayasan*) were created by the major military commands to act as holding companies for assorted business interests.

The Suharto Era (1965–98)

The charade of civilian supremacy played out under Sukarno gave way to blunt military dictatorship under General Suharto. In sharp contrast to the Sukarno era, however, this was a period of political stability and disciplined monetary and fiscal policies. Large amounts of foreign aid and private investment from the Western democracies helped the economy to grow at a brisk pace.

At the beginning of the Suharto era, the Indonesian economy was dominated by state-owned enterprises. These could be divided into six categories based on their legal status, one of which was "military enterprises."[4] Their comparative performance is unclear, however, because little information was made public about state-owned enterprises in general. Most likely, the differ-

3. Ironically, Suharto was dismissed from his position as commander of the Diponegoro Division in Central Java in October 1959 for demanding money from local businesses. Suharto was reassigned to the Army Staff College in Bandung (www.gimonca.com [November 18, 2006]).

4. The categories consisted of three distinct forms of central government enterprises (Persero, Perum, and Perjan), the state-owned petroleum monopoly (Pertamina) by itself, enterprises owned by provincial and local authorities, and enterprises owned by the military. Rieffel and Wirjasuputra (1972). A short and readable account of the evolution of TNI businesses up to the mid-1970s can be found in Crouch (1975/76).

ences were not great because military officers, both active and retired, managed many of the nonmilitary state-owned enterprises. For example, General Ibnu Sutowo consolidated Indonesia's oil and gas enterprises into the state oil company that became Pertamina in 1968 and was for many years ABRI's major "cash cow."[5]

Although military-dominated state-owned enterprises may have been the largest source of off-budget income in the Suharto era, most studies have indicated that private companies operating under foundations linked to the military were the dominant source.[6] Some of these were wholly owned by the military, but most were partnerships with local business leaders (often Indonesian-Chinese) or with foreign investors. They benefited from preferential access to bank credit, monopoly franchises, and impunity from violating laws and regulations.

ABRI's business activities probably reached their height in the mid-1980s.[7] During the last ten years of the Suharto era, ABRI businesses in numerous sectors were taken over or muscled out by members of the Suharto family and its business partners, including several prominent Indonesian-Chinese tycoons.

Counterintuitively, the military won little in the way of budget resources during the Suharto era. The reasons for this are complex but generally relate to the particular system of patronage and control developed by Suharto. By withholding budget funds, he gave military commanders a strong incentive to engage in income-generating activities. At the same time, his ability to grant or deny access to these activities fostered a high degree of loyalty and dependence among these commanders.

One of Suharto's important political legacies was Pancasila, a national philosophy originally enunciated by Sukarno in the fervor of independence and enshrined in the Preamble of the 1945 Constitution. Its "five principles" are nationalism, humanity (all humans have common characteristics), democracy (in the form of the tradition of deliberating until a consensus is reached), social justice, and belief in one Supreme Being. In 1985 Suharto declared Pancasila to be the sole foundation of the Indonesian state and required all sociopolitical organizations in the country to pledge allegiance to its principles.[8] Although annulled as a formal doctrine in 1998, Pancasila remains an

---

5. Samego and others (1998, pp. 76–77). The other leading cash cow of this era still in existence is BULOG (Badan Urusan Logistik, the state logistics agency).

6. See the studies listed in chapter 4, n. 2.

7. See Lowry (1996); and Singh (1996).

8. Friend (2003, pp. 31, 152).

object of allegiance for the TNI and a litmus test for political leaders (in a nation whose motto is "Unity in Diversity").[9]

The position of the Indonesian military on the eve of the Reformasi era can be summarized as follows:

—It had become the single most powerful institution in the country as a result of its historic role in the struggle for independence, its intervention in 1965 to "save" the country from communism (an atheistic philosophy and a threat to the social elite), and General Suharto's success in maintaining political stability and achieving rapid economic growth for more than three decades.

—That power, however, was being eroded by growing internal competition and diminishing popular support. The competition came primarily from members of Suharto's large family and their business partners, usually labeled "cronies." Popular support was declining because of the military's clumsy intervention in domestic politics and heavy-handed attempts to crush secessionist forces.[10] Toward the end of the Suharto era, the venality of the president's family and friends reached epic proportions, which reinforced public perception of the regime's corruption, collusion, and nepotism (shortened to KKN for *korupsi, kolusi dan nepotisme*).

—As steps were taken to build a functioning democratic system after 1998, public concerns about ABRI's lack of transparency and accountability, and its culture of impunity, mounted. Its role in society also came into question since it no longer needed to defend the country from internal threats. Furthermore, its operational readiness was poor, especially in terms of weapons and equipment, and its officer corps was lacking in the professionalism, morale, and technological know-how of its peers in other countries, which meant that it was not defending the country effectively against external threats.[11]

9. The evolving role of the military from independence in 1945 until the collapse of the Suharto regime in 1998 has been analyzed from various perspectives. Robison (1986) adopts a class approach, viewing the military as a fundamentally conservative force in Indonesian society serving to protect the bureaucratic elite rooted in the precolonial aristocracy. Robison's original analysis is updated in Robison and Hadiz (2004). Friend (2003) takes a cultural approach, highlighting the impact of Javanese culture on the postindependence development of the military and other institutions.

10. Two incidents that seriously damaged the image of the military were a massacre of pro-independence civilians in East Timor in 1991 and a July 1996 attack on the headquarters of the opposition party PDI-P, which was headed by Sukarno's daughter, Megawati.

11. A popular phrase capturing the public attitude toward the TNI was *pagar makan tanaman*, meaning "the fence eats the crops" (instead of guarding them).

The Reformasi Era (1998–)

In July 1997 a financial crisis erupted in Thailand when a loss of confidence in government policies triggered an abrupt outflow of private capital. Similar crises followed in Indonesia in October and in South Korea in November. As a result, the currencies of all three countries depreciated sharply, and their governments rushed to stabilize market sentiment. However, the macroeconomic policies they devised produced steep declines in national output and per capita incomes. Indonesia was hardest hit, as its crisis precipitated a turbulent regime change and a long period of transition.

In the early months of 1998, street demonstrations against the Suharto regime and its supporters grew larger and more frequent, with matters only made worse by the regime's response: on May 12, military or police personnel attempting to control a demonstration at Trisakti University in Jakarta shot and killed several students. In short order, the head of the Golkar party called for Suharto's resignation, key cabinet members quit, the military leadership agreed not to intervene, and on May 21 Suharto stepped down. He was succeeded by Habibie, who had only become vice president in March 1998 and quickly announced plans to hold new elections in 1999.

In a fateful move, Habibie also agreed to let the residents of East Timor vote on whether to remain in Indonesia under "special autonomy" in the hope of ending the insurgency that had been bubbling in that small province since it was annexed in 1976. The vote, taken in August 1999, was overwhelmingly against remaining part of Indonesia. Infuriated by the result, militia units linked to ABRI went on a rampage of killing and property destruction that horrified the world, arguably hammering the last nail in the coffin of military rule in Indonesia.

Ironically, Habibie did more to establish civilian control over the military during his nineteen months in office than either of his elected successors, Presidents Abdurrahman Wahid and Megawati Sukarnoputri (daughter of President Sukarno), did over the next five years.[12] In the 1999 elections, Habibie had the advantage of being the incumbent and the candidate of Golkar, the party that was created by Suharto and that skillfully managed his reelection six times. However, Golkar did poorly in the House of Representatives (DPR) elections in June 1999. PDI-P, led by Megawati, won the most seats. Four

---

12. Said (2006a, pp. 227–28). From the early days of Reformasi, civil society groups labored to promote civilian supremacy over the military. Numerous studies contributed to this effort and traced its progress. They include: Anwar (2001); Haseman and Rabasa (2002); Samego and others (2002); Bhakti (2003); Mietzner (2003); Sukma (2003); Rinakit (2005); Chrisnandi (2005); and Hafidz (2006).

months later, in the indirect election of the president by the People's Consultative Assembly (MPR), Wahid, the leader of one of the Islamic parties, outmaneuvered Megawati to claim the presidency and offered her the vice presidency, which she accepted.

The ill-fated tenure of President Wahid was distinguished by his deep commitment to democratic governance and social justice but was handicapped by his dysfunctional style of leadership.[13] He tried to reform too much too fast and committed several costly blunders. He was forced out of office in July 2001 when the military refused to obey his order to institute martial law to quell demonstrations against his government.

President Megawati served out the rest of Wahid's term but was unable to win the election of 2004. During her tenure, on the positive side, she appointed a remarkably strong cabinet, did not interfere excessively in economic policymaking, and restored a sense of political stability. In response, the economy moved onto a moderate path of growth, with GDP climbing at the rate of 5–6 percent a year. In addition, she supported a series of amendments to the constitution that greatly strengthened democratic governance, one of which called for the direct election of the president. On the negative side, Megawati's aloof style of leadership eroded her popular support and contributed to a growing suspicion of KKN reminiscent of that surrounding the Suharto regime. She also sought to build support within the military through appointments and other actions inconsistent with the three main objectives of Reformasi in the military area: civilian control, accountability, and professionalism.[14]

Even so, Megawati was unable to halt the antimilitary drift of the Reformasi era. The National Police was removed from military control in 1999, and the seats reserved for the military in the MPR were reduced from seventy-five before Reformasi to thirty-eight following the June 1999 election, then to zero following the April 2004 election. Law 34 of 2004 on the TNI, signed by Megawati just days before her term ended, formalized civilian control over the military and prohibited its involvement in political and economic activities. Article 76 of the law required the TNI to transfer all of its business activities to the government by 2009.[15]

13. He appointed Indonesia's first civilian minister of defense since the 1950s: Juwono Sudarsono. Said (2006a, p. 220).

14. All of Indonesia's civilian governments have worked to ensure that like-minded officers were appointed to key leadership positions in the TNI rather than making these appointments on the basis of merit. This practice has been a factor in creating a TNI that seems more political than professional.

15. These and another seventeen military reforms adopted under Reformasi are listed in a paper by Muhammad Asfar included in UNSFIR (2005).

Already in decline, the TNI's far-flung and loosely managed business empire suffered greatly in the financial crisis of 1997/98. Despite their privileged positions, many TNI-owned and controlled businesses went bankrupt. Most evidence suggests that the revenue generated by the TNI's business activities shrank steadily between 1998 and 2004.

On the eve of the parliamentary and presidential elections in 2004, the future role of the TNI in Indonesia's political and economic life seemed up in the air. Reforms in the military area after Suharto's departure in 1998 had been more superficial than substantive. The TNI remained committed to its territorial command structure, military personnel from top to bottom were moonlighting in an immense range of revenue-generating activities, and operational readiness was not perceptibly greater than it had been when Suharto stepped down. Furthermore, two of the strongest contenders for the presidency were former military generals: Susilo Bambang Yudhoyono, leading the newly established Democratic Party, and Wiranto, leading the resurgent Golkar Party. Chronologically, this narrative resumes in chapter 6 with the inauguration of President SBY. Chapters 4 and 5 focus on the range of the TNI's business activities and the TNI's off-budget revenues and expenditures, respectively.

4

The TNI's Current Business Activities

The first comprehensive study of Tentara Nasional Indonesia (TNI) business activities appeared in 1998. It was conducted by Indria Samego and a team of eight researchers based at the National Institute of Sciences (LIPI).[1] The study identified thirty-one distinct businesses linked to the army command, eight linked to the navy command, eight linked to the air force command, and ten linked to the police command, for a total of fifty-seven units. It was followed by a rich assortment of studies, some of which have attempted to refine or update the LIPI list, but none have produced what can be considered a definitive or authoritative list.[2] One of the most detailed lists, compiled by an Indonesian political risk consulting firm in 2003, identifies nine major TNI and National Police foundations and eighty-five of their affiliated companies.[3]

---

1. Samego and others (1998). Until LIPI was allowed to undertake this study, research on the TNI's business activities was off limits for Indonesian scholars. The first effort to construct an inventory of the TNI's business activities appears to be Rieffel and Wirjasuputra (1972).

2. Iswandi (1998); McCulloch (2000); Singh (2001); International Crisis Group (2001b); Basri (2001); Anggoro (2001); McBeth (2002); Widoyoko and others (2002); Tim Penelitian (2004); Nurhasim (2005); Sukadis and Hendra (2005); Working Group on Security Sector Reform in Indonesia (2005); Human Rights Watch (2006).

3. The nine foundations were the TNI headquarters' Yayasan Markas Besar ABRI (six companies), the army's Yayasan Kartika Eka Paksi (thirty-three), Kostrad's Yayasan Kesejahteraan Sosial Dharma Putera (twelve), Kopassus's Yayasan Kesejahteraan Korps Baret Merah, the navy's Yayasan Bhumyamca (eight), the air force's Yayasan Adhi Upaya (eight), the Ministry of Defense's Yayasan Kejuangan Panglima Besar Sudirman (ten) and its Yayasan Satya Bhakti Pertiwi, and the Police's Yayasan Brata Bhakti Polri (seven). See Van Zorge, Heffernan & Associates (2003, p. 12).

Most recent studies divide TNI business activities into categories. The LIPI 1998 report identified two categories, institutional and noninstitutional, to which Danang Widoyoko and his team added criminal activity in 2002. A study by the Working Group on Security Sector Reform in 2005 used two main categories, legal and illegal, and divided the first one into institutional and noninstitutional subcategories, which they further divided into direct and indirect activities.

None of these classification systems seem sufficiently rigorous. Therefore we have expanded on them to produce the system presented in box 4-1, the components of which are the subject of this chapter.

Formal Business Activities

The TNI's formal businesses are more or less visible to the public, and some have been reasonably transparent in their past operations. They consist of entities established under and governed by either the Corporation Law, the Foundation Law, or the Cooperatives Law.

Businesses under the Corporation Law

Businesses in this category are registered as corporations and are directly owned by the Ministry of Defense, the TNI Headquarters, or an individual military command. Ownership can consist of either a majority or a minority interest. No businesses of this kind appear to exist at the present time. Previous ones in this class may now be associated with foundations or cooperatives and thus fall into one of the next two subcategories.

Businesses under the Foundation Law

One of the first military foundations was Yayasan Pembangunan Territorium Empat (Foundation for the Development of the Fourth Territorial Command) established by Suharto in 1957 when he was the commander of the Diponegoro Division in Central Java. Military foundations were set up to manage the business activities of individual commands in response to the TNI leadership's concerns that the officer corps was losing its professional character as a result of its increasing involvement in income-generating activities. The declared and often repeated purpose of these foundations was to enhance the "welfare of soldiers" (*kesejahteraan prajurit*), implying an emphasis on low-ranking military personnel. They maintained a relatively low profile through the turbulent 1960s and the high-growth decade of the 1970s.

In the 1980s, however, their overall role in the Indonesian economy mushroomed, inspired by a number of high-profile foundations affiliated with

---

Box 4-1. A Classification of Military Business Activities[a]

Formal Activities
    Corporations operating under the Corporation Law
        Majority ownership interest
        Minority ownership interest
    Foundations operating under the Foundation Law
    Cooperatives operating under the Cooperatives Law
Informal Activities
    Security services
    Commercialization of state assets
    Special relationships with state-owned enterprises
    Owned or controlled by TNI-related persons
        Active military personnel
        Retired military personnel
        Family members of active or retired military personnel
        Cronies of active or retired military personnel
Illegal Activities
    Resource extraction (timber, sand)
    Toll collection (on movement of goods and people)
    Protection
    Smuggling
    Drugs, prostitution, gambling

a. Except where noted, the business activity is owned, controlled, or materially influenced by the Ministry of Defense, TNI Headquarters, or a TNI command or unit.

President Suharto's family members and their business associates. These foundations became a leading source of corruption, collusion, and nepotism (KKN). By the end of the decade, almost every government department and agency (including the Central Bank and Ministry of Finance) had established one or more foundations. Political parties, universities, private companies, and even nongovernmental organizations (NGOs) followed suit.[4] The corruption associated with both military and nonmilitary foundations in the 1980s was due in part to legal ambiguities. Since no laws had been passed to

4. According to a foreign defense attaché interviewed in Jakarta on September 1, 2005, individual graduating classes from the military academy have established foundations.

regulate the establishment and activities of foundations, they operated in somewhat of a legal limbo.[5]

By the time the financial crisis erupted in late 1997, the universe of military foundations was involved in every sector of the economy and every corner of the country. Its impact on efficient resource allocation was believed to be hugely negative. To cite a few of their questionable practices, they misused state assets (including natural resources), maintained national and local monopolies, and borrowed from banks for unproductive purposes.[6]

As Indonesia struggled to recover from the financial crisis, domestic and foreign experts alike gave high priority to the reform of foundations.[7] Reflecting this sentiment, the International Monetary Fund (IMF) made one of the conditions of its financial support the passage of a law requiring foundations to be transparent and accountable. Following a long and contentious debate, the House of Representatives passed Law 16 of 2001 on Foundations, which President Megawati signed on August 6, 2001, less than a month after she replaced President Wahid.

The Foundation Law may qualify as one of the worst pieces of legislation enacted since Suharto's departure in 1998. Within a year of its passage, an amendment was drafted to fix several glaring weaknesses. The parliament, however, did not get around to enacting the amendment (Law 28) until October 2004.

One key point is that the Foundation Law applies to all foundations, whether established by an individual, a profit-making company, an NGO, or a government body. The law contains no provisions that apply specifically to TNI-linked foundations or foundations in the public sector.

---

5. The Civil Code, inherited from the Dutch colonial administration, governed foundations before the Law on Foundations was enacted in 2001. Although the Law on Social Organizations enacted in 1985 applied to foundations, it related more to the political rather than financial/business aspects of their activities. An excellent overview of the legal framework for nonprofit, nongovernmental organizations in Indonesia can be found on the website sponsored by the U.S.-based Council on Foundations and the International Center on Non-Profit Law (www.usig.org). The section on Indonesia was drafted by, and is updated by, Bivitri Susanti, executive director of the Centre for Indonesian Law and Policy Studies.

6. The amount of nonperforming loans at the end of 2006 owed to Indonesian banks by business units under TNI foundations could be large and could represent a substantial claim on future budget resources.

7. An audit of foundations in the defense area carried out by the Supreme Audit Board (BPK) in 2000 found many problems, including loss of government assets, unexplained expenditures, and unauditable accounts. Specific recommendations for fixing these problems were conveyed to the Ministry of Defense.

Another key point is that the Foundation Law does not confer tax-exempt status on foundations, which are treated like other formally established private sector bodies for tax purposes. Thus foundations pay the government's payroll tax on the salaries of their employees, the sales/value-added tax on services provided for a fee, and the corporate income tax. All of this is rather murky, however, because the Foundation Law is silent on the subject of taxation, while Indonesia's various tax laws and regulations leave a lot open to interpretation.[8] The effect of this system is to create a powerful incentive for foundations not to make any profits, which is presumably done by inflating expenses to match revenues.

Weaknesses in the legal framework for foundations represent a large obstacle to transferring to the government business activities now owned or controlled by TNI-linked foundations. Even if the assets and liabilities of these foundations can be clearly and quickly discovered and disclosed, legal challenges could delay such transfers for years. Moreover, fixing the Foundation Law does not seem to be on the agenda of the government or the DPR, nor is there any visible public pressure for tighter implementation of the law as it now stands.

Businesses under the Cooperatives Law

Military cooperatives in Indonesia fit comfortably into the broad cooperative movement in Indonesia, which in turn is part of the global cooperative movement that originated in the late 1800s in Europe and the United States. Virtually every military command has a cooperative performing functions comparable to those of the Army and Air Force Service system of Post Exchanges (PXes) in the United States.[9]

As elsewhere, the heart of the cooperative movement in Indonesia lies in independent rural agriculture cooperatives, which date back to the colonial period. More specific to Indonesia is the prevalence of cooperatives linked to "host" organizations. Cooperatives currently exist in almost every central and

---

8. Message from Nono Makarim, September 3, 2006. It is also the case that contributions by individuals to foundations cannot be deducted from their income in determining their liability to the individual income tax. A group of leading Indonesian foundations is working to make these contributions deductible.

9. S. Yunanto and others compiled a list of TNI cooperatives in each of the thirty-one provinces in 2001. The totals they provide, based on information from the Ministry for Cooperatives, are: army, 923 cooperatives with 430,000 members; navy, 124 cooperatives with 126,000 members; and air force, 147 cooperatives with 42,000 members (membership in more than one cooperative is common). See Nurhasim (2005, pp. 52–58).

local government workplace, as well as in most private companies with more than fifty employees.

Cooperatives were mentioned explicitly in the original Constitution of 1945. Article 33, in the section on social welfare, states: "The economy shall be organized as a common endeavor based on the principles of the family system." The elucidation of this article states: "The form of enterprise that meets those conditions is the cooperative."

Law 12 of 1967 replaced colonial-era regulations governing cooperatives and was itself updated by Law 25 of 1992. Consistent with the basic principles of the cooperative movement globally, current law specifies that the purpose of a cooperative is to advance the welfare of its members, membership is voluntary, management is democratic (one vote per member), and the net income is divided among the members in proportion to their individual activity.

Military cooperatives in Indonesia conform to these principles to a high degree with two exceptions. First, they are hosted by a command-and-control organization with top-down decisionmaking. Accordingly, the commanders of military units are able to engage a cooperative linked to their unit in activities that the members might choose to decline and can invest the net income of this cooperative without regard to the views of its members. Second, a number of military cooperatives have become substantial business conglomerates that appear to be serving the commands to which they are attached more than their members.

Like cooperatives in other sectors, military cooperatives form a hierarchy with three levels: primary, secondary, and central (*primer, sekunder, induk*).[10] Simplistically, primary cooperatives are made up of units at the lowest levels of command, secondary cooperatives are regional associations of primary cooperatives, and central cooperatives are associations of secondary cooperatives.[11] Each service has a central cooperative.

The most important distinction between foundations and cooperatives is that the former do not have members. Foundations exist to advance the pur-

10. At the end of 2004, the air force, for example, had 137 primary cooperatives (Primkopau), 12 secondary cooperatives (Puskopau), and the central cooperative (Inkopau, whose members consisted of the 12 Puskopau plus the Primkopau of the Air Force Headquarters Command). See Fathoni (2005, p. 125).

11. To illustrate the scale of cooperative activities, the net income of the central cooperative of the air force, Inkopau, was Rp 12 billion ($1.3 million) in 2004. Of this amount, Rp 6.6 billion ($700,000) was reinvested in new activities, Rp 4.1 billion ($450,000) was added to reserves, Rp 547 million ($60,000) was used for management and staff compensation, Rp 547 million ($60,000) was used for educational activities, and Rp 274 million ($30,000) was used for social activities. Fathoni (2005, p. 132).

poses spelled out in their charters, which must be related in some fashion to social welfare.[12] Another distinction is that under the Cooperatives Law the government has an important role in promoting and strengthening cooperatives, derived from the Constitution of 1945 and reflected in the creation of a cabinet post for cooperatives in 1960, currently the minister of state for cooperatives and small and medium enterprises. While the Ministry of Justice and Human Rights is responsible for registering foundations, it has no comparable responsibility or capacity to monitor their activities.

Informal Business Activities

This category consists of lawful activities that for various reasons are not reflected in the budget. It has four subcategories, two of which—"security services" and "commercialization of state assets"—would be on the budget if the existing laws and regulations relating to government financial management were strictly enforced. Specifically, Law 20 of 1997 on Non-Tax Revenue requires that 100 percent of the non-tax revenue generated by the activities of any central government entity, including the Ministry of Defense and the TNI, be deposited in the government's Treasury account and that all expenses incurred in generating this revenue be met by debiting the government's Treasury account.[13] Since all four subcategories involve informal activity, even less reliable information is available about their scale or scope than exists for the TNI's "formal" business activities.

Security Services

Revenue associated with the provision of security services became a prominent issue at the end of 2005 as a result of a *New York Times* report about Freeport-McMoRan Copper & Gold's mining operation in Papua.[14] According to this report, Freeport-McMoRan was paying millions of dollars a year directly to military and police units assigned by the government to provide security for its mining operation. Freeport-McMoRan has indeed been disclosing these payments in the financial statements it is required to file with the

12. A staff member of the Centre for Indonesian Law and Policy Studies remarked that "foundations are owned by their purpose." Under Law 16 of 2001, when a foundation is terminated its remaining assets must be transferred to another foundation with a similar purpose or to the government. Interview, December 13, 2006.

13. Inquiries about the non-tax revenue of the Ministry of Defense and the TNI yielded contradictory information.

14. Jane Perlez and Raymond Bonner, "The Cost of Gold, The Hidden Payroll: Below a Mountain of Wealth, a River of Waste," *New York Times*, December 27, 2005, p. A1.

U.S. Securities and Exchange Commission, which are therefore a matter of public record. It has rejected the implication in the report that these payments in any way violated U.S. or Indonesian laws and has stressed that it is adhering to the U.S.-U.K. Voluntary Principles on Security and Human Rights. The full story may never be reliably documented, but one fact beyond dispute is that none of these payments have been reflected in the government's budget.

Another interesting case concerns the ExxonMobil project at the Arun gas field in Aceh province, which started exporting liquefied natural gas (LNG) in 1977. TNI units were tapped to provide security for the project because of its inherent vulnerability and its location in a conflict zone. The defense perimeter established by the TNI was called "the ring of steel," and Pertamina (the Indonesian national oil company, and ExxonMobil's partner in this project) made substantial payments to the TNI to obtain its support.[15] Pursuant to the peace agreement between the Indonesian government and the GAM (the leading secessionist organization) in 2005, the TNI units guarding the Exxon-Mobil project were withdrawn. Presumably the payments from Pertamina stopped at the same time. It is not clear how the TNI adjusted to this sudden and substantial loss of revenue.

A third notable case arises from the Tangguh LNG project under construction by BP in the Bird's Head region of Papua. From the beginning, this project has sought to be a world-class model for extractive industries in socially and environmentally sensitive locations. To this end, the project adopted an innovative approach called Integrated Community Based Security, under which the project provides its own security force, backed up by the National Police in accordance with guidelines contained in a formal agreement with the provincial chief of the National Police. The agreement also includes guidelines for joint requests from the project and the National Police for TNI support in exceptional circumstances. Financial transparency, one of the key features of the project, is reflected in an explicit arrangement stipulating that the Indonesian government's Executive Agency for Upstream Oil and Gas Activity (BP MIGAS) must fully disclose payments to the National Police for security provided to the project.[16]

15. Interview with a security adviser in Jakarta, December 12, 2006. Van Zorge, Heffernan & Associates reported in 2003 that the ExxonMobil LNG facility in Aceh was paying Rp 50 billion ($5 million) each year to the TNI and National Police for security. Van Zorge, Heffernan & Associates (2003, p. 14).

16. The project is monitored closely by the Tangguh Independent Advisory Council, which issued its fourth report on the project in March 2006. See www.bp.com/liveassets/bp_internet/indonesia/STAGING/home_assets/-downloads/t/TIAP_report_March_2006.pdf.

It is easy to get lost in the details of the Freeport-McMoRan, ExxonMobil, and BP cases, and others. From a policy perspective, the essential point is that no payments currently being made by mining companies (and other extractive industries) to TNI or National Police units are reflected in the government's official accounts, which means that laws governing the financial operations of agencies are not being respected.[17] If anecdotal evidence is any indication, many TNI units are providing security services for both foreign and domestic companies, and even for some local governments.

Presidential Decree 63 of 2004 on the Protection of Vital National Objects mandates the involvement of the TNI in the protection of "Vital National Objects." This decree created a body (the Manager of Vital National Objects) to be responsible for ensuring the security of all such objects, which include the Freeport-McMoRan operation along with most other large oil/gas and mining operations. It gave the National Police primary responsibility for protecting these objects and assigned backup responsibility to the TNI. As of mid-2006, however, the necessary implementing regulations had not been issued.

Commercialization of State Assets

As in the case of foundations and cooperatives, commercialization of state assets is endemic throughout the public sector. It would be hard to find a single substantial central government ministry or agency that does not generate some revenue from the use of land or equipment that it owns or controls.[18] Little if any of this revenue appears to be reflected in the budget, despite Law 20 of 1997 on Non-Tax Revenue.

Like all other government bodies, the TNI presumably derives the bulk of its revenue from this subcategory through the lease or sale of land, as in the case of the golf course built on the Halim Air Force Base outside of Jakarta. At the time of the 1997–98 financial crisis, it stood out among enterprises managed by the air force for being relatively unaffected, with profits in excess of Rp 100 billion ($8 million) a year.[19] Another well-known source of land-based revenue in Jakarta is the shopping mall anchored by a Carrefour supermarket. The commercialization of state assets subcategory encompasses

17. In the first quarter of 2006, the Minister of Defense was quoted as saying that a policy was being formulated on security services, but no signs of such a policy have appeared since then.

18. In many government buildings, for example, space is leased for commercial bank branches, snack bars, barber shops, and the like.

19. Gabriel Sugrehetty and Anari Karina, "Sejak Dulu ABRI Berbisnis," *Tempo* Magazine, no. 12/27, December 1998, pp. 26–27.

many small-scale activities as well, such as renting meeting halls for weddings and renting trucks to private businesses.[20]

Special Relationships with State-Owned Enterprises

As noted in chapter 3, TNI officers on active duty were put in charge of many of the foreign businesses nationalized in the late 1950s. Although TNI leadership in this sector is clearly not the only factor, the history of state-owned enterprises in Indonesia is rich in scandals and poor in financial results. The Indonesian government's large portfolio of state-owned enterprises is a legacy of the strong socialist-nationalist sentiment at the time of independence, whipped into a froth by Sukarno. It remains visible today in the broad resistance to selling off the numerous enterprises still owned by the government.

Pertamina stands out among state enterprises with a military link both because of its size and because of its historic connections to the TNI. It was largely a creation of General Ibnu Sutowo, who took charge of several precursor companies and transformed them into a powerful monopoly widely regarded as the TNI's principal cash cow in the 1960s and 1970s. In 1975, however, as a result of excessive borrowing in foreign currencies, Pertamina had to be bailed out by the Central Bank and General Ibnu was forced to resign.[21] He was succeeded by several more army generals, until a civilian CEO was appointed in 1989. Even so, it can be assumed that the TNI still has a special relationship with Pertamina.[22]

One other prominent state-owned enterprise linked to the TNI is BULOG, the state logistics agency. It is responsible for stabilizing the price of basic commodities such as rice and sugar.[23]

Today, state-owned enterprises linked to the TNI generally offer three kinds of benefits: they provide employment for retired military officers and their

20. In 2005 TNI Commander Endriartono Sutarto was quoted to the effect that the TNI's business activities would be turned over to the government within two years, after which there would be no more trucks from military cooperatives "carrying sand to build hotels, malls, and apartment buildings." See *Koran Tempo*, April 14, 2005, from Salim Said (2006a, p. 238).

21. For more details, see Samego and others (1998, pp. 61–62); and Widoyoko and others (2002, pp. 20–22).

22. In December 2006, President SBY appointed former TNI commander Endriartono Sutarto as the chairman of the board of directors of Pertamina, reportedly with a mandate to stop the smuggling of fuel out of Indonesia. In January 2007, the head of Pertamina raised the possibility of floating an initial public offering of stock by the end of 2008. This step would put considerable pressure on Pertamina to develop a more arm's-length relationship with the TNI. See John Aglionby, "Indonesia Oil Group Calls for Modest Flotation," *Financial Times*, January 25, 2007.

23. For more details, see Widoyoko and others (2002, pp. 22–23).

family members, enter into noncompetitive contracts with companies linked to the TNI, and sell goods and services to the TNI either above or below market prices. This subcategory of "special relationships with state enterprises" would disappear with strict enforcement of existing government laws and regulations, which would require all state enterprises to meet high standards of governance, transparency, and accountability.

Business Activities Owned or Controlled by TNI-Related Individuals

This is not only one of the most opaque subcategories of TNI business activity but also one that has received an enormous amount of press and scholarly attention. The LIPI team, for example, devotes almost an entire chapter of its book to six business conglomerates associated with six former generals, starting with Ibnu Sutowo.[24] The book lists sixty-eight subsidiaries of these conglomerates that were active in 1998 and describes the operations of many of them. An equal number of undocumented subsidiaries may have existed at that time. [25]

Presumably because most of its research was carried out before Suharto was forced to resign, the LIPI study did not cover what was generally considered the largest military-linked conglomerate in the 1990s: Suharto, Inc. This is the informal term applied to the extensive business interests of President Suharto's family members and close friends. However, it is more accurate to view Suharto, Inc., as a collection of conglomerates rather than a single one.[26]

In the mid-1990s, the combined value of Suharto, Inc., companies and the other military-linked conglomerates was reported to be several billion dollars. The money used to build these companies came from monopolies or franchises granted by the government, preferential access to credit from the banking system, and special deals with private sector domestic and foreign partners (such as equity interests in exchange for facilitating investments). Anecdotal evidence suggests that the TNI "share" of the profits of these businesses has declined steadily since 1998 and may be quite small now. The subcategory of business activities owned or controlled by TNI-related persons will disappear as these entities gradually become like other private companies,

24. Samego and others (1998).

25. A list developed by S. Yunanto and others consisting of twenty-seven major shareholders of companies linked to the TNI can be found in Nurhasim (2005, p. 45).

26. Two of Suharto's children, in particular—his eldest child, Siti (Tutut) Hardijanti Rukmana, and his fifth child, Hutomo (Tommy) Mandala Putra—built extensive business empires on the basis of their privileged status. Typically, they would be given an equity interest in a new company without making any material contribution, or a loan to finance their equity share would be repaid with compensation for serving as a director.

do business with the TNI at arm's length, and do not share profits with any TNI command.

"Large-scale" business activities controlled by the families and friends of active TNI personnel are not the only challenge in ending business activities controlled by individuals related to TNI personnel. An equally complicated challenge is how to handle the "small-scale" businesses that a high percentage of TNI officers, NCOs, and ordinary soldiers engage in to supplement their official salaries. These businesses run the gamut from food stalls and beauty parlors to transportation services and consulting companies. It is hard to draw a line between those that constitute "harmless" moonlighting activities and those representing serious conflicts of interest. While these activities appear to violate the TNI Law, requiring TNI personnel to abandon them would be futile and probably counterproductive.

Illegal Business Activities

The last category of TNI business activities—illegal ones—is a black box. It contains five subcategories: resource extraction, toll collection, protection, smuggling, and the social crimes of gambling, prostitution, and drugs. Although the government and military leadership have always ascribed this behavior to rogue individuals acting in direct violation of orders, military personnel are rarely arrested, tried, and convicted for engaging in them. It can be assumed that quite a few of these "rackets" are passed from one unit commander to the next as officers are reassigned and promoted.

In the subcategory of resource extraction, much has been written about TNI-linked companies in the forestry sector involved in logging, sawmill operations, or plywood factories. It is reasonable to assume that some if not most of these companies also engage in a certain amount of illegal logging and exporting on the side.

As is well documented, TNI personnel have also participated in toll collection in conflict areas such as Aceh. Net revenue to the TNI from this source is probably diminishing as a result of competition from the National Police, the far-reaching decentralization of power to the district level at the beginning of 2001, and investigative reporting by today's remarkably free press. It is likely to be more common in regions with weak governments.

In the subcategory of protection, a somewhat subtle distinction can be made between "informal" security services that the TNI openly provides to private companies and governmental bodies and illegal "shakedowns" threatening violence to persons or damage to property. Although some of this kind of activity presumably continues in some places, it appears to be on the decline, and the income it generates is probably small.

Smuggling has the honor of being the activity that launched off-budget financing in the independence struggle sixty years ago. Apart from the smuggling of tree logs, mentioned earlier, the biggest source of income in this category may be fuel smuggled from the domestic market, where it is heavily subsidized, to neighboring countries. The government has started reducing the fuel subsidy, however, and as the price differential shrinks, the volume of smuggled fuel will surely shrink as well.

Income the TNI obtained in the past from social crimes (gambling, prostitution, and drugs) appears to be gravitating to the National Police.

The Bottom Line on the TNI's Business Activities

The overarching reality is that the business activities of the TNI are in a state of flux. The evidence available at the beginning of 2007 points to the following preliminary conclusions:

—The TNI continues to have considerable power in the Indonesian political system, much of which derives from the money available to the TNI (broadly defined) from its off-budget business activities.

—The practice of generating off-budget income is deeply ingrained in the culture of the TNI and Indonesian society in general. Although individual active and retired military leaders have spoken out in favor of getting out of business, and the TNI's new doctrine seems to reinforce this change, there is no evidence that a significant faction of the officer corps is pressing for reforms in this area.

—Some legally and politically complex issues stand in the way of transferring the TNI's *formal* businesses to the government. For example, the assets of military foundations that appear to belong to the TNI may in fact belong to "founders," creditors, or other third parties.

—Putting the TNI's *informal* business activities (especially commercialization of assets and security services) on the budget could yield a significant increase in non-tax revenue for the central government and could become a model for other ministries and agencies.

—It will take more than a generation to wean the TNI from *illegal* activities. Progress in this area could be more rapid than for the civil service generally, but only with exceptional leadership from senior TNI officers.

5

The TNI's Off-Budget Revenues and Expenditures

Two fundamental questions about the business activities of Tentara Nasional Indonesia (TNI) have yet to meet with satisfying answers, even from the minister of defense or the TNI commander: how much money is generated and what is this money used for? We approach these questions by examining the "conventional wisdom" about the TNI's off-budget funding and then estimating the amount of income from formal, informal, and illegal business activities in 2006, along with the share of this income available "for operational purposes." We also examine two other off-budget sources of income that are distinct from the TNI's business activities, as we define them, but are probably larger—gifts and procurement commissions.

Conventional Wisdom

According to the most widely cited estimate, the TNI obtains 70 percent of its funds from off-budget sources and 30 percent from the central government's budget. For decades, analysts and scholars have either adopted this ratio or offered variations ranging from 55:45 to 75:25.

Perhaps it is not necessary to look further than a statement by Juwono Sudharsono in 2004, before he became minister of defense for the second time: "The proportion of government to non-government budget over the years is variously estimated by foreign and domestic analysts, ranging from 30–40 percent funding from government, and correspondingly 70–60 percent independently funded."[1] Although he attributed this breakdown to others,

1. Sudarsono (2004, p. 25).

he did not dispute it and appeared to endorse it. Nor has he subsequently offered a different estimate.

While Minister Juwono's statement is clear, efforts to probe its basis quickly yield two quite different interpretations, which also arise in connection with other estimates. One interpretation is that the funds provided in the defense budget represent only 30 percent of the TNI's "requirements" in order to be fully operational. By implication, the remaining 70 percent simply is not available, which explains why the military's operational readiness is so low. This account of the 70:30 split is often put forward by senior TNI officers, although without much conviction and without any evidence. Nevertheless, it points to an important question: what is the "gap" between the funds provided by the defense budget and the amount required to "fully fund" the TNI? No one has yet produced a solid analysis of the size of this gap. We address this question in chapter 8.

The second interpretation is that the 70:30 split compares the gross revenues of various TNI business activities with budget funds presumably spent entirely "for operational purposes." But these are apples and oranges. First, the bulk of the gross revenue is used to meet the expenses of the TNI business units that are generating the revenue. The only funding from these units available "for operational purposes" is their net income or profit and some of this net income is diverted "for nonoperational purposes." Second, some portion of the TNI's budget allocation is also diverted "for nonoperational purposes." In other words, the various ratios that have been put forward have little meaning because they are based on undefined terms. They are more smoke than substance.

A more rigorous approach is to distinguish clearly between gross revenue and net income, and between income used "for operational purposes" and income used for "nonoperational purposes." In our study, gross revenue is equivalent to sales proceeds before subtracting any expenses. Net income is equivalent to profit after taxes. This distinction is conventional and consistent with normal business accounting concepts. By contrast, our use of the term "for operational purposes" is unique to this study.

We divide the expenditure of the TNI's off-budget income into four categories, the first two comprising spending "for operational purposes": (a) spending for the "welfare of the soldiers" in the form of salary supplements or housing/education/health benefits that can be considered "normal" compensation to supplement substandard compensation from the budget; and (b) spending to procure weapons, equipment, and services to support military operations mandated by the government. Spending in the other two categories is nonoperational: (c) "excessive" compensation to military personnel in cash or in kind (for example, luxury cars); and (d) kickbacks or "profit-sharing" with relatives or friends or other nonmilitary partners.

Gross Revenue and Net Income

The difference between the TNI's gross revenue and net income is large, and it varies systematically from category to category. For the TNI's formal businesses, expenses are relatively large and therefore net income tends to be small. For the TNI's informal business activities, expenses can be relatively high for security services (the soldiers employed as private guards receive extra pay) and relatively low for commercialization of assets (rents are simply collected and deposited in a bank account). For the TNI's illegal activities, we assume expenses are zero because the TNI is accepting mostly cash in return for remaining inactive.

To estimate the gross revenue and net income of the TNI's *formal* business activities, we start with figures from Van Zorge, Heffernan & Associates for 2003, which put the combined annual revenue from all business activities of the TNI and the National Police at Rp 1 trillion ($100 million) and the combined annual profit at Rp 500 billion ($50 million).[2] We adjust these estimates by removing the National Police share, dividing them among our three categories of TNI business (formal, informal, illegal), and assuming a decline from 2003 to 2006. Since Van Zorge, Heffernan & Associates describe their estimates as "surely not an exaggeration," we adopt these figures as the low end of plausible ranges and double them to establish the high ends (the precise adjustments for this and all other estimates presented in this chapter can be found in appendix B).

We then run a cross-check, based on the "book value" (net worth) of the individual business units of the TNI foundations and cooperatives on the list of 356 foundations and cooperatives and their related business units provided to us by the Ministry of Defense in December 2006.[3] Taking the extreme values from each calculation yields a range of Rp 420 billion to Rp 1.35 tril-

2. Van Zorge, Heffernan & Associates (2003, pp. 10–11). An informal World Bank review of eighty-eight companies under eight military foundations put their combined gross revenue at Rp 2.9 trillion ($320 million) in 1998 or 1999. World Bank (2000, p. 29).

3. As an example of the squishiness of even these numbers, they do not appear to include any cash or real property assets of the foundations themselves, or any of their outstanding liabilities, such as bank loans. The numbers relate only to the business units under the foundations, some of which are wholly owned and some of which are partly owned, and some of which are "leased."

Figure 5-1. *Gross Revenue and Net Income of TNI Business Activities, 2006*
Millions of U.S. dollars

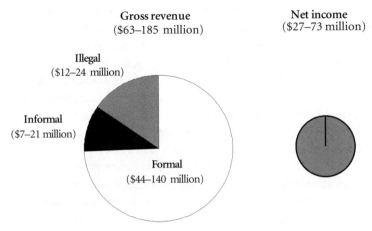

Gross revenue
($63–185 million)

Net income
($27–73 million)

Illegal
($12–24 million)

Informal
($7–21 million)

Formal
($44–140 million)

lion ($44 million to $140 million) for gross revenue and Rp 80 billion to Rp 270 billion ($8 million to $28 million) for net income of the TNI's *formal* business activities in 2006.

Using similar calculations, we arrive at estimates of the TNI's informal and illegal business activities (also described in appendix B). When the three components are added together, gross revenue totals Rp 610 billion to Rp 1.79 trillion ($63 million to $185 million), and net income Rp 270 billion to Rp 714 billion ($27 million to $73 million), as shown in figure 5-1.[4]

Uses of Net Income

Clearly, much confusion about the TNI's off-budget revenue arises from the failure to distinguish between gross revenue and net income. Another important distinction commonly overlooked is between funds used for operational and nonoperational purposes, with operational uses being further divided

---

4. In an interview on January 12, 2006, a retired general with extensive knowledge of the TNI's business activities told us that these activities currently generate several hundred billion rupiah of funding, but less than Rp 1 trillion ($100 million). Adding our estimates of net income for formal, informal, and illegal business activities yields a figure of Rp 270 billion to Rp 714 billion ($27 million to $73 million). This suggests that our estimates may be too low by at least 15 percent.

into spending for the minimum welfare of the soldiers and spending for supplies and equipment.

The rationale for putting minimum welfare under "operational" spending is that official salaries and allowances, financed by the central government budget, are generally considered too low to support a decent standard of living. Commanders unable to supplement the compensation of the soldiers under their command would not be able to count on the readiness of their units. Many soldiers would be moonlighting to make ends meet, would be in poor health because they could not afford medical care and pharmaceuticals, or would desert. In short, some of the supplemental compensation funded by off-budget revenue is critical to operational readiness.

The same rationale applies to commanders and officers at all levels. Their official salaries are not sufficient to meet the basic needs of military families with their social status. However, it is impossible to draw a line between justified and "excessive" supplements in an objective manner. It could be argued, for example, that the government should provide every unit commander with a mobile phone because the landline network is insufficient to ensure operational readiness. At the other extreme, providing generals with luxury model cars cannot be justified on the grounds of operational readiness. Drawing on anecdotal evidence, we have arbitrarily divided the uses of the TNI's net income from business activities in 2006 into 40 percent "for operational purposes" and 60 "for nonoperational purposes" (see figure 5-2).

Nonbusiness Off-Budget Funding

Another point that tends to be overlooked is that income from business activities (as we and most other analysts and reporters define them) may not be the major source of the TNI's off-budget funding. Two other sources are equally large by our estimates: gifts and procurement commissions.

Making gifts to people in authority is a deeply embedded cultural practice in Indonesia, and the TNI is a beneficiary at least to the same degree as the civil service in general, if not more so.[5] The higher the rank and the more important the command of the recipient, the more numerous and larger the gifts. These gifts are usually unsolicited and often unrequited, which makes it hard to call them bribes or a form of business income. At the same time, almost all come from businesses that have some kind of commercial relationship with the recipient. Such gifts are made both in cash and in kind. A

---

5. A common term for these gifts is *sogokan*, which is often translated as "bribe" but has a more neutral connotation in Indonesia.

Figure 5-2. *Sources and Uses of Net Income of TNI Business Activities, 2006*
Millions of U.S. dollars

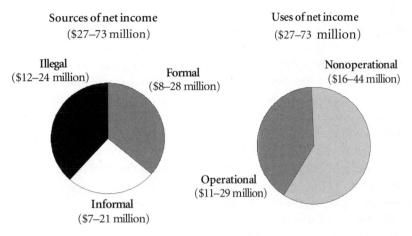

Sources of net income
($27–73 million)

Uses of net income
($27–73 million)

Illegal
($12–24 million)

Formal
($8–28 million)

Nonoperational
($16–44 million)

Operational
($11–29 million)

Informal
($7–21 million)

sergeant posted in a village might receive a couple of chickens, or a goat, or some clothing. Gifts to officers might take the form of a television set, a motorcycle, plane tickets for a weekend in Singapore, cash to help finance a daughter's wedding, a new car, or a VIP package for the pilgrimage to Mecca.

One important subcategory of gifts is payments by regional governments from their own budgets. Anecdotal evidence suggests such payments have become quite common, but we have omitted them from our estimates because a substantial portion may be for specific security services, which would put them in the category of informal business activities.

Another significant subcategory may be payments made to gain entry to the TNI as ordinary soldiers or cadets or to obtain a specific posting, which are considered normal practice for anyone without connections (such as a close relative serving with the TNI). It is considered normal for senior officers to "purchase" a posting to a "wet" position with well-developed sources of off-budget funds. Senior officers even pay for the privilege of attending Staff and Command School.

Procurement commissions, less politely referred to as kickbacks, are the other large source of nonbusiness, off-budget income available to the TNI. The conventional wisdom is that 30 percent of the budget funds allocated to ministries and agencies "leaks" out, meaning it is not spent for its intended purpose. Some of this can be justified for operational efficiency in an environment where official compensation is generally considered inadequate. In some cases, the leakage is more of a diversion than a kickback.[6]

Nevertheless, the most common form of leakage across the entire government is the kickback.[7] An office director with a budget allocation of Rp 100 million ($10,000) to procure some new computers will select a vendor who will deliver computers worth Rp 90 million ($9,000) to the office and Rp 10 million ($1,000) to the director. This is an example of a small-scale kickback. Allegations of large-scale kickbacks are frequently reported in the media. The ones related to procurement from foreign sources, using foreign exchange earmarked in the budget, are considered especially lucrative.

The amounts of off-budget income in the form of gifts and procurement commissions are far from clear, but it is plausible that both are correlated with the level of procurement by the TNI. According to our calculations (see appendix B), the TNI's income from gifts and procurement commissions totaled Rp 1.2 trillion to Rp 2.4 trillion ($130 million to $260 million) in 2006, while the amount available "for operational purposes" was about Rp 300 billion to Rp 600 billion ($31 million to $62 million).

Total Funds Available

Figure 5-3 illustrates our estimate of the TNI's nonbusiness, off-budget income, how it relates to the funds generated by the TNI's business activities, and how both sources together relate to the defense budget. According to our figures, the TNI's nonbusiness activities (gifts and procurement commissions), as we define them, generate more off-budget income than the TNI's business activities (formal, informal, and illegal). Added together, they point to off-budget income available for operational purposes of Rp 408 billion to Rp 872 billion ($42 million to $91 million) in 2006. This off-budget income is equivalent to only 1.5 percent to 3.0 percent of the defense budget for 2006—a rather small fraction.

---

6. For example, an office may receive Rp 100 million ($10,000) to procure new equipment and furniture, and the office director in Jakarta may divert Rp 10 million ($1,000) to a special fund used to pay a transportation subsidy to clerical workers facing long commutes by public transportation from neighborhoods with affordable housing. Structured as an amount paid only on days the workers come to the office, the subsidy reduces absenteeism and improves productivity in the office.

7. Ironically, we are focusing here on a source of off-budget funds that actually comes from the budget. We treat it as off-budget funding because it is not transparent and can be used freely by the recipients (in the case of the TNI) either for operational or nonoperational purposes.

Figure 5-3. *Off-Budget Income of the TNI and the Defense Budget, 2006*
Millions of U.S. dollars

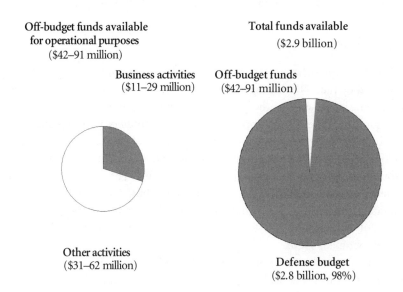

Off-budget funds available
for operational purposes
($42–91 million)

Business activities
($11–29 million)

Other activities
($31–62 million)

Total funds available
($2.9 billion)

Off-budget funds
($42–91 million)

Defense budget
($2.8 billion, 98%)

Future Trends

In formulating policies both for ending the TNI's business activities and for putting the TNI fully on budget, it is obviously important to have a sense of the trends, not just a snapshot of the income for an isolated year. As of this writing, we see no evidence pointing to increases in any of the five major sources of the TNI's off-budget income that we have considered. The question is how fast are they likely to decline in the next five years?

In our estimation, income generated by the TNI's formal business activities (under foundations and cooperatives) is likely to decline rapidly, even to zero by the end of 2009, in response to Article 76 of Law 34 of 2004. Income generated by the TNI's informal business activities (primarily security services and the commercialization of state assets) is apt to decline slowly, perhaps 5 percent a year, more or less in lockstep with the process of putting these sources on budget throughout the government. Income from the TNI's illegal business activities will probably decline at a somewhat faster pace, 10 percent a year, as this business continues to migrate to the National Police, as subsidies that encourage smuggling are reduced, and as law enforcement improves. The other two sources of off-budget income (gifts and procurement commissions) are likely to decline at the rate of 5 percent a year, depending largely on the extent to which governmentwide reforms dampen the incentive to give government officials gifts and make it harder for them to obtain kickbacks on supplies and capital equipment procured with budget funds.

Expenditures

Although attempts have been made to calculate the revenue and net income generated by the TNI's business activities, little has been said about how the net income is used. One of the most sophisticated efforts, by Yunanto and others, simply identifies six categories of spending—"soldiers' welfare, education, health, social activities, contributions to TNI Chief of Staff or other high-ranking military officers, distribution of budget deficit"—but without further elaboration or mention of other possible categories.[8] For example, anecdotal evidence suggests that TNI personnel have contributed to political parties or candidates running for government positions. It has not been possible in the course of our study to arrive at a better breakdown of how the TNI's off-budget income is spent.

In the future, the social pressure on the TNI to maintain these extrabudgetary expenditures is likely to diminish as compensation for government employees across the board increases and civil service reforms take hold. Until the demand for these funds begins to shrink, however, TNI commanders will have an incentive to continue engaging in business and nonbusiness activities that generate off-budget funds.

Concluding Remarks

At some point in the past, 70 percent of the TNI's funds may well have come from off-budget sources and 30 percent from the central government budget. Today, however, the shares appear to be very different. In our estimates, the off-budget income available to the TNI for operational purposes in 2006 was in the range of Rp 408 billion to Rp 872 billion ($42 million to $91 million), which translates to only 1.5 to 3.0 percent of the defense budget for that year. The small size of this figure is a product of several factors:

—Because of the decentralized nature of the TNI's business activities, there is no single source of reliable data or credible estimates to arrive at an aggregate figure. To produce a credible estimate, it would be necessary to analyze the activities of several thousand distinct commands, foundations, cooperatives, and companies, plus the activities of several thousand individual active

8. Nurhasim (2005, p. 49).

and retired defense personnel (ordinary soldiers and noncommissioned officers, as well as commissioned officers).

—While some income generated by lower-level commands is presumably shared with higher levels, lower-level commands have powerful incentives against fully reporting to senior commanders the actual amounts of off-budget income they obtain.

—All previously published estimates of the TNI's off-budget gross revenue and net income are based on anecdotal information or unpublished sources. Even the Supreme Audit Board (BPK) audits and an audit carried out by Ernst & Young at the request of the TNI commander do not fully meet modern standards of accuracy.

—Distinguishing funds used "for operational purposes" from funds used "for nonoperational" purposes is a critical step. By our estimates, less than half of the TNI's off-budget funds are used for "operational purposes." This category consists of spending that is essential to the operational readiness of TNI units. It can be divided into spending for low-ranking soldiers, spending for high-ranking soldiers, and spending for the procurement of expendable supplies and capital equipment. Funding used for nonoperational purposes consists of "excessive" compensation for senior officers (beyond the compensation required to ensure operational readiness) and funds shared with family members, friends, and business associates of military personnel.

—By our estimates, only 30 percent of the off-budget income available for operational purposes comes from the TNI's business activities. Seventy percent comes from unsolicited gifts and procurement commissions (kickbacks).

—The business activities of the TNI suffered heavy losses in the 1997–98 financial crisis. Income generated by these activities has almost certainly fallen steadily since the beginning of Reformasi in 1998. We expect the net income from the TNI's formal business activities to fall to zero or close to it by 2009 and the net income from the TNI's informal and illegal business activities to continue to fall.

Are our estimates robust? Most emphatically not. They are very crude approximations. We have, however, clarified considerably the full range of analytical categories that would have to be examined to produce a robust estimate. We challenge others to come up with better estimates. We also caution that the effort required to produce better estimates at this time would probably outweigh the value of the results. We see few policy choices that depend critically on accurate estimates of the TNI's net income from business or its other sources of off-budget, nonbusiness funds. If an assumption is necessary, then a good one is that the TNI's off-budget funds will be zero in the near term because that is the policy objective spelled out in Law 34 of 2004, and the one most consistent with a professional military fully funded by the central government's budget.

In any case, we hope our estimates will not get in the way of our central message, namely that ending these business activities and putting the military fully on budget is an exceedingly complex process and cannot be accomplished by 2009, except in the narrowest fashion. Furthermore, the pace of progress in this area will be determined primarily by the pace of civil service reform generally (because there is little evidence that the TNI will be a pace-setter), and by the rate of growth of the Indonesian economy. The faster the economy grows, the more room there will be for the government to raise public sector compensation and reduce reliance on off-budget revenue-generating activities.

It would also be a mistake to believe that rapid economic growth and bold public sector reforms will wean the TNI completely from its off-budget sources of funds in the near term. The cultural patterns that generate these funds are ingrained in the society. It will probably take at least one generation (twenty years) for these patterns to change enough to defuse the issue for the Indonesian government or for countries interested in supporting the modernization of the TNI.

6

From Starting Point to Finish Line

Law 34 of 2004, which provided for transferring the TNI's business activities to the government, was enacted in early October. Two weeks later, Susilo Bambang Yudhoyono (SBY) was sworn in as Indonesia's sixth president. These two events mark the starting point, point A, for the reforms that are the subject of this policy study. Point B is the twin goals of ending the TNI's business activities and putting the TNI fully on budget by 2009. The policy challenge is to get to point B from point A. This chapter focuses on the issues surrounding the first part of the goal: the withdrawal of the TNI from its extensive business activities. The issues relating to full funding are taken up in chapters 7 and 8.

Article 76 and the 2009 Objective

Article 76 was introduced late in the legislative debate over Law 34 of 2004. It was added to the chapter containing transition provisions, and followed only by two procedural articles.[1] Article 76 is emphatic, at least on the surface:

1. Within 5 (five) years of the enactment of this law, the government must take over all business activities owned or controlled by the military either directly or indirectly.

2. The procedures and regulations for implementing paragraph (1) will be set forth in a Presidential decree.

1. The government's draft of the TNI law did not include an article on military business. A competing draft proposed by an opposition party member of the House of Representatives Commission I included the provision that became Article 76, but with an earlier deadline. The 2009 deadline was adopted as a compromise.

A first step in implementing Article 76 was taken at the beginning of 2005 but not disclosed publicly. Defense Minister Juwono Sudharsono formally instructed the TNI commander to prepare a list of TNI business activities considered to be eligible for transfer to the government. The first visible implementing action came at the end of August 2005, when an interministerial team was formed to resolve issues related to the implementation of Article 76 and to draft the required presidential decree. The designated chairman of the TNI Business Takeover Team (Tim Supervisi Transformasi Bisnis TNI, or TSTB TNI) was Said Didu, secretary of the Ministry of State-Owned Enterprises, and it included members from the Ministries of Defense, Finance, and Justice and Human Rights.

At the end of September 2005, the TNI produced a list of 219 military businesses, which it turned over to the TNI Business Takeover Team.[2] Six months later, statements and documents from Ministry of Defense officials referred to a list of 1,520 distinct TNI business units, but none of the units on either list were publicly disclosed.[3] In December 2006, the Ministry of Defense provided us with a list of 23 military foundations with 107 affiliated business units (*badan usaha*), and 172 military cooperatives with 54 affiliated units, for a grand total of 356 business units.[4] Therefore as of the beginning of 2007, the public had received no official information about the identity of the individual business activities of the TNI.

The Takeover Team produced a preliminary draft of the presidential implementing decree in the first quarter of 2006 and discussed it with a few nongovernmental military experts. A major concern of these experts was that the draft focused narrowly on the establishment of an agency (Badan Pengelola Transformasi Bisnis TNI, or TNI Business Management Agency) to manage the businesses taken over from the TNI. The draft failed to define business activity and appeared to cover only the "formal" TNI businesses on

2. According to a Ministry of Defense letter to Human Rights Watch in December 2005, the group of 219 entities consisted of 25 foundations, 89 companies under foundations, and 105 cooperatives engaged in business. Human Rights Watch (2006, p. 27).

3. The government's intentions became cloudier shortly afterward when Defense Ministry officials and others involved were quoted to the effect that only 10 or so of the 1,520 TNI business activities were sufficiently attractive to be transferred to the government, and that most of the 1,520 units were small-scale activities and therefore would remain with the TNI.

4. Most of the business units are in the form of corporations (P.T.). Quite a few are educational establishments (from kindergartens to universities), and some hospitals and banks appear on the list. Incomplete information is provided for about sixty-five of the units, perhaps because they are inactive. Another twenty-five are designated as being "leased out." Note, too, that the list does not include the Ministry of Defense's own foundation and its affiliated business units.

the list delivered to the Ministry of Defense the previous year. The draft was also ambiguous about whether the businesses transferred to the new agency would be retained indefinitely or disposed of, and how any revenue accruing to the agency from the operation or sale of these businesses would be used.

In June 2006, there were credible reports that the presidential decree would be issued before President SBY's traditional address to the nation on August 16, substantially in the form of the initial draft from the Takeover Team. At the end of July, however, a disagreement surfaced in the press between the minister of defense, who was recommending that the TNI businesses be transferred to an existing asset management company under the Finance Ministry, and the minister of finance, who objected to the move.

The president made no mention of the much-delayed implementing decree before or during his August 16 speech. However, on October 26, 2006, a news item posted on the TNI website reported that the team's draft decree was in the hands of the State Secretariat, noting further that a takeover of thousands of military businesses in China had been completed smoothly in a period of six months with the help of an increase in the military's budget to offset the loss of income from these businesses. The TNI, the item added, expected to facilitate the transfer of its businesses to the government as soon as the defense budget was increased enough to offset the loss of business revenue and fully meet the welfare needs of the soldiers.[5]

In mid-December, we were informed by a senior official in the Ministry of Defense that a fundamentally different approach had been adopted and would be disclosed soon. In place of a presidential regulation (Peraturan Presiden) directing the transfer of TNI businesses to the new TNI Business Management Agency, a presidential decision (Keputusan Presiden) would be issued creating a National Team to manage the disposition of TNI businesses. This team would report directly to the president and have three components:

—A Guidance Team (Tim Pengarah) at the ministerial level to provide broad policy guidance.

—A "Supervision Team" (Tim Pengawas) at the secretary general level to approve operating policies and specific actions to be taken.

—An Executive Team (Tim Pelaksana) to oversee the day-to-day operation of the transfer process, recommend specific policies and actions, and manage the businesses transferred to the government.

The agencies represented on the Guidance Team and the Supervision Team would be the same as those represented on the TNI Business Takeover Team created in 2005. Unlike the TNI Business Management Agency, which would

5. See www.tni.mil.id/news.php?q=dtl&id=113012006112378 (November 18, 2006).

have been closely linked to the Ministry of State-Owned Enterprises, however, the Executive Team would be an independent body headed by a reputable person with extensive experience in business restructuring.

Issues Related to the TNI's Business Activities

As pointed out in chapter 2, the TNI is not unique in generating revenue from off-budget activities. Virtually every agency at every level of government is involved in such activities. This practice plus six other policy issues merit the government's close attention in the takeover process.

ISSUE 1

What general policy will the government adopt and enforce toward the business activities of government agencies across the board?

Government agencies from the center to the village level obtain off-budget funds through foundations, cooperatives, and other means. Strictly speaking, at the central level at least, keeping these funds out of the budget process is unlawful. According to Article 23 of the Constitution of 1945 (as amended): "The state budget . . . [shall] be implemented in an open and accountable way." Law 17 of 2003 on State Finance says that "state finance will be managed in an orderly manner, based on the provisions of laws, efficiently, economically, effectively, transparently, and responsibly to produce a sense of justice and decency" (Article 3(1)). It also states: "All receipts that become the right and outlays that become the obligation of the state in the budget year concerned must be included in the National Budget (APBN)" (Article 3(5)).

Under Law 20 of 1997 on Non-Tax Revenue, the income from business activities of government agencies is defined as non-tax revenue that must be reported to the Ministry of Finance quarterly and included in the national budget. In addition, Law 1 of 2004 on the State Treasury requires that all receipts and outlays of the state must be executed through the State's General Bank Account. This is interpreted to mean that agencies are required to deposit gross receipts and pay costs related to these receipts by debiting the State's General Bank Account.

Given these clear and strict requirements and the prevalence of business activities by offices throughout the public sector, why is it so hard to find receipts from such transactions in the budget, apart from the dividends paid by state-owned enterprises? One answer, neatly captured in a recent report on "fiscal transparency" by the International Monetary Fund, is that "the lack of reporting on off-budget activity is the main area of weakness" of the central government across the board. The report specifically mentions the TNI:

> Foundations and cooperatives are widespread and their extrabudgetary activities are not covered by general government statistics.... Many have characteristics that would require their inclusion in general government, as it is well-established that state assets and personnel are directly used. Foundations are also widely used as a means of supplementing line ministries' budgets, particularly those of the Indonesian Armed Forces (TNI) and police, but also reportedly for other ministries.[6]

The government has a clear but difficult policy option in this area. Nothing in the foundation or cooperative laws prohibits government-sponsored foundations and cooperatives from reporting their receipts and outlays to the Ministry of Finance so that they may be included in the budget. The government could issue regulations that clarify the obligations of government-sponsored foundations and cooperatives in this regard, establish penalties for noncompliance, and enforce these regulations.

An important precedent could be set in the process of implementing Law 34 of 2004 on the TNI (see issue 7). The government has chosen to divest military foundations and cooperatives of the formal businesses they own and transfer these to a body controlled by the Ministry of Finance or the Ministry of State-Owned Enterprises or the president's office. If this were done in an efficient manner, it would provide a basis for removing similar businesses from the foundations and cooperatives of other government agencies and bringing them on budget.

ISSUE 2

How will government policies with respect to military foundations be changed?

The basic law on foundations (Law 16 of 2001) is weak in a number of areas, especially transparency. For example, it has been interpreted to preclude the auditing of military-sponsored foundations by the Supreme Audit Board (BPK), although no such prohibition is made explicit in the text.[7]

Reflecting a chronic weakness, the government has not yet issued implementing regulations for Law 16. Article 71 requires existing foundations to

---

6. IMF (2006, p. 6).

7. A BPK audit in mid-2000 recommended that the Ministry of Defense issue clear management guidance and separate foundations from command structures.

come into compliance within five years of the law's enactment, but that requirement has little meaning without implementing regulations.

We believe that a critical first step in cleaning up the military foundations is to distinguish between foundations in the public sector and foundations in the private sector, even though Law 16 of 2001 makes no such distinction. We define public sector foundations as those that are founded by and serve to support public sector ministries and agencies and enterprises. By contrast, most foundations in the private sector are small organizations engaged in socially useful and economically efficient activities.[8] Ninety percent of the governance problems associated with foundations occur in the public sector. Military foundations are the most prominent members of this group and may account for as much as one-half of the money that flows through public sector foundations annually.

A second step is to treat foundations in the public sector as "money-laundering" entities, not in the criminal sense, but in the more general sense of a means to conceal sources of funding and allow managers to spend funds in a discretionary manner.[9] To be clearer, public sector foundations obtain funds primarily in the form of dividends from affiliated business units and contributions from businesspersons having a commercial relationship with the sponsoring public sector agency. Unlike the typical foundation in the United States and other advanced democracies, virtually none in Indonesia obtain funds from ordinary individuals with an interest in the foundations' missions. Indonesia's public sector foundations exist for the benefit of the sponsoring agency, not for the general citizenry or a specific social goal. The beneficiaries of the foundations linked to the Ministry of Finance, for example, are the employees of the Ministry of Finance, not the taxpaying public. These foundations do not conduct research or educational activities designed to arrive at a more efficient tax system. They simply redistribute income from wealthy people to people with military, police, or bureaucratic power.

One of the strongest recommendations in this study is that Indonesia adopt a governmentwide policy for government-sponsored foundations that meets global standards of good governance. As a precursor to a governmentwide policy, a smart move could be to target military-sponsored foundations and call for full disclosure of the directors, managers, supervisors, statutes, and annual reports of these foundations. Selective audits by BPK would help to

---

8. A number of foundations associated with the Suharto family became quite large and were associated with some of the worst rent-seeking activities, but they have a low profile now and do not seem to be major sources of corruption.

9. Our finding is based on anecdotal information, but no other explanation is plausible.

ensure that audits by certified public accountants are rigorous. Another important step could be to make military foundations independent of the commands they are supporting by requiring a majority of their directors to be civilians and the top manager to be an experienced business or NGO professional with no military background.

A compelling rationale for preserving foundations in the public sector does not exist, whereas the case for closing them down in the short term is strong. However, one practical reason for not closing them right away is the practice of making gifts to military commanders, which is likely to persist over the next five years at least. Channeling these gifts to transparent foundations rather than having them remain as discretionary funds for military commanders would be a major step toward a professional military establishment.[10]

In the medium term, the case for closing all of the foundations linked to the Ministry of Defense and the TNI rests on several points:[11]

—Their contributions to the welfare of low-ranking soldiers are marginal and easily met by a relatively small increase in the defense budget.

—After their profitable business units have been transferred to the government, they will not have enough financial assets to provide meaningful contributions to military welfare.

—The time senior officers spend in managing these foundations diverts attention from their core military responsibilities.

—To the extent that it makes sense to have foundations supporting military personnel generally, it would be better to depart from past abuses by establishing new foundations with better defenses against corruption, collusion, and nepotism (KKN).

Indonesia already has a state-owned enterprise created in 1991 to provide pension and insurance benefits to military personnel (including the National Police and civilian employees of the Ministry of Defense): P. T. Asabri (Asuransi Sosial Angkatan Bersenjata Republik Indonesia). Participation is mandatory and premiums are automatically deducted from salaries.[12] Unfortunately, despite the mandate in its charter to provide a range of high-quality services, P. T. Asabri's record of financial management is poor or worse.

As a first step in addressing the foundation issue, the government could commission an objective study of TNI-linked foundations to quantify and assess the contributions they are currently making to the welfare of low-

10. An interim step could be to keep the TNI headquarters foundations and the three principal service foundations, and to merge all the others into these four foundations.

11. The same arguments apply to foundations linked to the National Police.

12. Government Regulation 67 of 1991.

ranking soldiers. It would also be useful to estimate the cost of putting these contributions on budget.

How will government policies with respect to military cooperatives be changed?

Like the foundation law, the cooperative law of 1992 falls short of meeting the transparency and accountability standards associated with good governance in today's world. Here also, the government faces a fundamental choice of either amending the law or adopting a special policy for cooperatives composed of military or civilian employees of the government (including local government). And here again, the government could begin by targeting military cooperatives as a step toward a broader policy that would eventually be reinforced by amending the cooperative law.

Unlike foundations, public sector cooperatives in general or military cooperatives in particular have no serious disclosure problems. Most of the military cooperatives post their operating results publicly at least once a year. Shutting down military cooperatives across the board would serve no useful purpose. At the same time, in the interest of good governance it would be desireable for the Ministry of Defense to identify and classify the cooperatives, collect basic financial data on their operations, and make recommendations for changes in policies and procedures that would improve members' benefits while reducing the role of military personnel in their management.

A discretionary approach seems the most appropriate method of dealing with the handful of military cooperatives that have become large business enterprises staffed in part by active-duty military personnel. Some of these large-scale cooperatives may own businesses that should be transferred to the government because they originate from or depend on state-owned assets.

What policy will the government adopt on the provision of security services by military units?

The range of security services provided by the TNI is unclear, the amount of revenue generated by these services is not reported, and government policy in this area remains murky. As mentioned earlier, the TNI's off-budget security activities made the front page of the *New York Times* in a 2005 report on the Freeport-McMoRan Copper & Gold mining operation in Papua. While critics of Freeport tend to treat this as a simple black or white issue, it is dev-ilishly complex. To begin with, the Freeport operation is one of the largest sources of government revenue. Any interruption of its operations would have an immediate, direct, and adverse impact on the budget deficit, which the government is trying to reduce. Security on this mine site is a serious concern, owing to a history of attacks by separatist groups, intrusion by illegal miners, and questionable behavior by TNI personnel. Dozens of mining and oil sec-tor operations across the country, as well as many large manufacturing and infrastructure projects undertaken by domestic and foreign investors, have arranged to obtain some degree of security protection from the TNI.

Security services provide a superb example of the government's struggle to reconcile the realities on the ground with its desire to improve transparency and accountability. A logical first step to this end would be to enact laws that establish rules and procedures and assign responsibilities for enforcement. Laws passed thus far seem to assign primary responsibility for security services to the National Police, but some provisions leave the door open for the TNI to be involved. Another problem is that in many parts of the country the National Police do not yet have the capacity to provide effective security against immediate and significant threats.

Putting the revenue from security services on budget is a simple matter in theory. Fierce resistance to this step is to be expected, however, for all of the obvious reasons. Simply stopping the practice of making military personnel available for security services is not practical either. For one thing, security is a serious matter in most places where the TNI is engaged in this business, and effective substitutes for TNI personnel are not readily available. For another, this activity provides a useful function for soldiers who might otherwise be idle or engage in socially disruptive activities.

Another point to note, security services are not an issue for the entire pub-lic sector. The principal competing sources for this business at the present time are the TNI and the National Police. One policy option is to encourage private companies to carry more of the burden of providing security ser-vices.[13] Another option could be to transfer TNI personnel to the National Police and retrain them to work in collaboration with the security forces of private companies.

---

13. The SATPAM system of private security guards was established in 1980 and now num-bers more than 200,000 guards, including 90,000 in Jakarta. These are commonly hired to guard office buildings and factories. "The system was established to give police control and to demobilize several competing security companies established by retired military and police officers." International Crisis Group (2001a, p. 7).

A number of reliable security firms already exist, most founded or managed by retired military officers. These firms could expand by recruiting from the ranks of military personnel, helped by early retirement incentives. This option would have the advantage of reducing the military payroll, thereby creating room to increase military compensation or to recruit new personnel more suited to highly skilled military tasks. Article 15 of Law 2 of 2002 on the Police authorizes the National Police to "issue operational licenses to, and carry out supervision over, companies in the field of security services." However, a law specifically geared to the regulation of private security services could help to make private security companies carry more of the burden.

A study of "legitimate" security services provided by TNI units would be a logical next step for the Ministry of Defense. Such a study could examine alternative approaches for engaging TNI units in security services, such as formalizing them in contracts between clients and the Ministry of Defense and putting the associated revenues on budget.

ISSUE 5

What policy will the government adopt on the commercialization of state assets owned or controlled by military units?

An important step in putting the income from the commercialization of state assets on the budget would be to provide easy public access to an inventory of land owned by the central government along with information about the agency responsible for the use and development of each parcel and whether it has been leased to a third party. In addition, the BPK could produce a baseline audit of the use of government land and equipment. Without waiting for a governmentwide initiative, the Ministry of Defense could also sponsor a study of the commercialization of state assets by the Ministry and the TNI.

As 2007 began, the government appeared to be ignoring both this category of military business and the security services category as sources of off-budget income. As long as it continues to do so, its implementation of Article 76 of Law 34 of 2004 can only be characterized as half-hearted.

ISSUE 6

What policies will the government adopt with regard to military involvement in illegal or criminal income-generating activities?

The biggest obstacle to reducing the military's illegal/criminal business activities is the decentralized and entrepreneurial manner, deeply rooted for decades, of supplementing its budget resources. Officers who have demonstrated skill in extracting income from legal and illegal activities have been rewarded with promotions and assignments to "wet" commands in the past. Young officers see the tangible benefits of this behavior and aspire to the same benefits as they gain seniority.

Strategies for reforms in this area can start at the top or the bottom, or from both at the same time. The current approach seems to be more ad hoc than strategic and mostly top-down, with an emphasis on moral suasion. President SBY was elected in part for his commitment to clean government and appears to have set a good example personally by appointing persons of integrity to his cabinet and supporting a wide range of anticorruption initiatives. Even so, progress has been slow in the face of bureaucratic resistance (especially from the TNI and police), and the electorate's general impression is that corruption remains well above acceptable levels.

A more bottom-up approach would be to give low-ranking public-sector employees (including the military) a substantial salary increase and to punish violators at all levels in a prompt and credible fashion. In fact, salaries are being raised. Punishing violators effectively runs against the grain of Indonesia's social conventions.

Although the public's cynicism regarding illegal and corrupt practices is not unwarranted, it may be excessive. Experience elsewhere in Asia provides some basis for optimism, not in the short term but over the next ten to twenty years. Indonesians may also underestimate the advantage they derive, compared with countries like Thailand and Vietnam, from having a remarkably open society (measured by freedom of speech and related freedoms of expression).

ISSUE 7

What approach will the government take to implementing Article 76 of Law No. 34 of 2004?

The basic policy choices for implementing Article 76 are between a broad and a narrow approach, and between a quick and a slow approach. Under a broad approach, all TNI business activities as classified in chapter 4 would be included in the implementation process. Under a narrow approach, only the private corporations (P.T.) wholly or partially owned by the TNI, either directly by military commands or indirectly through TNI-sponsored foundations and cooperatives, would be included. The scope could be narrowed further by excluding businesses that fall below a specified threshold (for example, for gross revenues or assets).

Under a rapid approach, the government would complete the transfer of all military businesses (either broadly or narrowly construed) by the Article 76 deadline of December 31, 2009. Under a gradual approach, the government would either ignore the deadline or formally extend the deadline to a later date. For more than a year the TNI leadership has been claiming that it will have all of its business activities transferred to the government by April 2007, thereby beating the official deadline by more than two years.[14] Realistically, however, it could only be met by defining business activities narrowly.

At the beginning of 2007, the government seemed to be moving in a relatively narrow and rapid fashion. This choice may be wise because it can yield tangible results in the near term. However, it defers the resolution of a number of fundamental reform issues in this area and may not achieve the sense of progress and credibility the government is aiming for.

The List of Business Activities

A great deal of skepticism still surrounds the government's intentions toward TNI business activities. Recall that the number of business units (*badan usaha*) was first announced as 219, then raised to 1,520, and then dropped to 356.[15] Furthermore, the government has failed to disclose any part of these lists. Experience over the past fifty years in many parts of the world provides a compelling reason for disclosure, namely to minimize asset stripping.

In the case of the TNI's business activities, asset stripping has been endemic for decades and represents a main reason for their poor performance. A burst of asset stripping from TNI enterprises probably occurred during the 1997–98 financial crisis when many viable businesses suddenly became unviable. Following the passage of Law 34 of 2004, it can only be assumed that the pace of

14. See, for example, Government of Indonesia, Ministry of Defense (2006, p. 2).

15. For each business unit, the December 2006 list includes information on its main sectors of activity (construction, transportation, education, and so on), its "book value" (undefined and undated), and the TNI's ownership interest (wholly owned, partial shareholding, and the like). The list does not include the Ministry of Defense's own foundations and its affiliated business units.

asset stripping in military-owned and -controlled business activities increased.[16]

Whatever the total value of the assets of TNI businesses in October 2004, it could easily have fallen by half at the end of 2006 and is likely to fall further by a large amount during 2007. Without any steps to reduce asset stripping, the value of all of the TNI's formal businesses could be negligible by the 2009 deadline specified in Article 76 of Law 34. This could in fact be the optimal strategy for ending the TNI's involvement in formal business activities.

The Transfer Process

As mentioned earlier, the latest plan for implementing Article 76 being pursued at the end of 2006 centers on creating an independent National Team reporting directly to the president to manage the takeover process. Here, as elsewhere, the devil is in the details, but information about the new approach is too meager to assess its likely effectiveness. To qualify as a bold approach, it would have to include most of the following steps: (a) disclose publicly the entire list of TNI business units to be transferred to the government, or a substantial part of the list; (b) issue a regulation or decree that freezes the assets controlled by these units and establishes penalties for violating the freeze; (c) establish an agency empowered to take possession of TNI business units and dispose of them expeditiously rather than manage them indefinitely; (d) spell out whether the proceeds of sale or liquidation will be added to the government's general revenues or whether they will be earmarked for some specific purpose; and (e) clarify the government's intentions with respect to the TNI's off-budget income flowing from security services, commercialization of assets, and other informal sources of income.

16. Anecdotal evidence includes the widely reported sale of the shares of Bank Artha Graha held by the Army's Yayasan Kartika Eka Paksi to private parties. It remains unclear how the proceeds were distributed. Also Mandala Airlines, owned in large part by the Kostrad command's Yayasan Dharma Putra, was sold in 2006 through a nontransparent process.

PART II

Fully Funding a Professional TNI

7

Designing a National Defense and Security Strategy

Without a clear national defense and security strategy, it is impossible to assess how much budget support the TNI needs to fulfill its missions. As explained in this chapter, twelve major policy issues will have to be addressed in the process of designing and implementing a credible strategy. They are numbered in sequence with the issues discussed in chapter 6. Without examining the availability of budget resources and evaluating key cost components of the defense budget, it is impossible to identify a feasible time path to the goal of full funding. Issues related to the defense budget are examined in chapter 8.[1]

The Current Policy Vacuum

In the first eight years of the Reformasi era, the government has issued only one national defense strategy document: the Defense White Paper of 2003.[2] Quickly characterized in Jakarta as a "half-hearted reform," it did not have a visible impact on the military budget in any subsequent year and appeared to be more a product of the TNI leadership than the civilian government.[3]

We cannot stress too much the difficulty of producing a study such as this one in the absence of a defense and security strategy developed by the civil-

---

1. Andi Widjajanto and Edy Prasetyono make three important points about defense strategy: (1) the first step is to define the threats in detail; (2) the resources of the government to support a defense force are always limited; and (3) defense strategy is never permanent, it must evolve. Widjajanto and Prasetyono (2006, pp. 1–2).

2. Government of Indonesia, Ministry of Defense (2003).

3. "TNI's Halfhearted Reform," *Jakarta Post*, April 15, 2003. Cited in Sebastian (2006, p. 150).

ian government and endorsed to some extent by the House of Representatives (DPR) or accepted by the TNI. At the same time, producing a credible strategy may be beyond the analytical capacity of any institutions or groups outside of the TNI. The best feasible alternative may be a strategy that represents a giant step forward from the 2003 White Paper and is considered halfway credible.

A TNI press release in October 2006 announced that the Ministry of Defense would soon be publishing the "Strategic Defense Review 2005" and the "Defense White Paper 2006."[4] While this news confirmed that a framework for the budget process was under consideration, sources inside the ministry predicted that it would not become publicly available until after the beginning of 2007. In his address to the nation in August 2006, President Susilo Bambang Yudhoyono (SBY) had this to say about the regime's plans for the TNI and the nation's defense, which can be seen as an overview of the strategy likely to emerge:

> The TNI is currently making efforts to strengthen and simultaneously enhance its capability, in its organization, in the professionalism of its personnel, and in its armaments.
>
> Much progress has been made in the effort to reactivate various armaments, which have previously been inoperable due to the lack of spare parts. We have also taken measures to procure new weapon systems on a gradual basis, proportional to the capacity of the budget. Defense cooperation with friendly countries continues to be increased, including cooperation in the development of our defense industry. It is our wish that in the future we shall be able to meet our own needs in the procurement of various main weapons systems.
>
> We do not intend to enlarge our current forces. What we wish to build is an essential force that we deem strong enough and able to secure the entire sovereign territory of our nation. Our defense is focused on guarding our sea and land boundary areas, particularly the outermost islands, including setting up security posts of the TNI.
>
> In addition to providing education and military training, we pay serious attention to the welfare of the soldiers, so that they are ready at any time and able to perform their duties to defend the nation and state. We continuously try to increase the salary, food allowance, old-age pension, and housing for our soldiers.

4. See www.dmc.dephan.go.id (October 3, 2006).

Policy Issues Related to Designing a Defense and Security Strategy

To begin our examination of the policy issues the government will have to resolve in the process of defining the objective of full budget funding, we focus on six issues related to designing a national defense and security strategy and follow up with six implementation issues.

ISSUE 8

What are the main external threats and what priority should be attached to each one for the purpose of determining the TNI's force structure?

While the threat of a conventional attack appears negligible at the present time, some minimal capacity to repel such an attack is an accepted feature of national sovereignty. Maintaining this capacity has the added benefit of creating trained personnel and units that can participate in regional defense arrangements and international (UN-approved) peacekeeping operations.

A minimal defense capacity consists of surveillance technology and interdiction forces. The surveillance technology includes ground radar, airborne radar, satellite, and sonar. The interdiction forces comprise attack aircraft, frigates/corvettes, submarines, short-range missiles (launched from air, ship, and mobile land platforms), and mobile strike forces. At the beginning of 2007, Indonesia fell substantially short of having this minimal defense capacity. Furthermore, the funds required to create such a capacity in less than five years appear to be well beyond the budget the government might be able to provide without reordering the country's national priorities.

The most serious external threats at present are related to the unlicensed exploitation of Indonesia's maritime and forestry resources. As noted in chapter 2, foreigners enter Indonesian territory freely to poach fish, and a large volume of timber is smuggled out of the country. Indonesia's maritime borders are among the longest in the world, and its land borders on Kalimantan, Papua, and Timor are almost impossible to control because of the mountainous jungle terrain.

Two other serious external threats are international terrorism and piracy, but both have a domestic component. As the world's most populous Muslim-majority nation, Indonesia has become a major focus of attention next to the hotbeds of terrorism in the Middle East, especially after four major terrorist attacks on Bali and in Jakarta between 2002 and 2005 targeting Australians and Americans. The response has been encouraging, with the National Police demonstrating a new pride of mission and the government cooperating actively with the United States and other countries leading the war against international terrorism. The TNI has played a supporting role in this area and has also used the issue to justify maintaining its territorial command structure. However, a clear and durable division of responsibilities between the TNI and the National Police has not yet been articulated. Moreover, the arguments advanced for giving the TNI a major role in combating terrorism in the future have not been compelling.

In the case of piracy, the security of the Malaka Strait is a global concern, and a stronger argument can be made for giving the TNI a major role here. As with terrorism, the piracy problem is as much domestic as external. Most of the pirate attacks in the Malaka Strait in the past decade (and for much longer, probably) appear to have been carried out by Indonesians from bases on Indonesian territory.

While Indonesia joined in bilateral patrols of the Malaka Strait with Malaysia and Singapore in 1992, meaningful cooperation only began in 1999, largely in response to Japanese concerns and offers of assistance. The three countries launched coordinated sea patrols in 2004 and coordinated air patrols in 2005. In addition, bilateral antipiracy training exercises have been conducted with the Japanese Coast Guard, and a U.S.-funded training program for the maritime units of the National Police has been initiated.[5] In the wake of these efforts, pirate attacks dropped from thirty-eight in 2004 to twelve in 2005 and six in 2006.[6] A modest near-term objective could be to raise the operational capacity (equipment and manpower) of the Indonesian forces involved in this narrow task to the more advanced level of Malaysia and Singapore.

ISSUE 9

To what extent will Indonesia participate in regional security arrangements?

As noted under issue 8, Indonesia's role in regional security is now focused narrowly on piracy in the Strait of Malaka. If at some point in the future the Association of Southeast Asian Nations (ASEAN) creates a security force that uses compatible equipment and engages in joint training and joint operations, this could sharply reduce the force Indonesia alone would need in order

---

5. Percival (2005, pp. 17–24).

6. From the website of the International Maritime Bureau's Piracy Reporting Center (www.icc-ccs.org/prc/overview.php).

to deal with smuggling, fish poaching, terrorism, piracy, or conventional attacks. To participate in such a force meaningfully, however, it would have to make a substantial investment in equipment and training and provide continuing budget support above the current level. As the largest ASEAN country, Indonesia is in the best position to champion the development of an ASEAN security force, but nationalist sentiments within Indonesia as well as within other leading ASEAN countries represent a significant political obstacle.

ISSUE 10

Will the national defense and security strategy be threat-based or capacity-based?

A threat-based national defense and security strategy is one in which the level of budget support is determined by the nature of the threats and the force structure required to deal with these threats. In a capacity-based strategy, the level of support is determined by the amount the government is prepared to provide and the operational capacities of the existing force structure. It can be assumed that a threat-based strategy requires considerably greater funding than a capacity-based strategy, although the choice here is not between all and nothing. The Ministry of Defense has argued for maintaining a "minimum essential force," which implies a somewhat more ambitious strategy than a purely capacity-based strategy.

While a large increase in the TNI's share of the central government budget seems unlikely in the next five years, the scope for increasing the budget as a whole (with a bigger pie) is significant. If Indonesia were to launch a robust military reform program, the potential for a bigger slice for the TNI could be even greater (see chapter 8, issue 21, on the growth of the military budget over the next five to ten years).

ISSUE 11

What will be the respective roles of the TNI and the National Police (Polri) in dealing with threats to public order from domestic terrorists, regional rebellions, and communal violence?

The allocation of budget funds between the TNI and the National Police will depend on their precise responsibilities in dealing with internal threats and also on the efficiency with which each force uses the funds it receives. Currently, the operational capacities of both forces are weak. One immediate policy challenge, as the government's revenues grow, will be to decide whether to give the next Rp 1 trillion available for internal security to the National Police or the TNI.

Indonesia's internal threats can be grouped under two headings: threats to public order and threats to natural resources. Threats to natural resources are addressed under issue 12. Major threats to public order—regional rebellions, communal violence, and terrorist attacks—are not a common occurrence in most countries, whereas they have been a problem in Indonesia since independence. Furthermore, while internal security is the responsibility of the police force in most countries, the TNI has played the leading role in addressing these threats for the past sixty years. By almost all accounts, after seven years of reforms and capacity building, the National Police alone still cannot deal effectively with these three major threats. The policy choices for addressing them differ somewhat.[7]

REGIONAL REBELLIONS. The peace agreement reached in 2005 with the secessionist movement in Aceh seems likely to hold. The only other significant threat of secession appears to lie in Papua. The government may be underestimating the difficulty of crushing the nascent independence movement there.

Papua will be a major test of military reform and there are some encouraging signs. However, the incentive to abuse power for financial gain is immense because of the value of Papua's resources and the inability of the Papuans to protect these resources by themselves. Over the past forty years, the most visible TNI "business" activity there has been the provision of security services for Freeport-McMoRan's huge mining operation. But the TNI's power in Papua is unrivaled, and there is evidence that the military has been involved in illegal logging and other illegal activities for decades. Scaling back the TNI's presence and profile could be a smart move. One risk of doing so, however, is that organized crime will mushroom. Another serious risk is that the resulting power vacuum will encourage separatist sentiment. The policy issues here are especially complex and critical.

COMMUNAL VIOLENCE. The arguments for reducing the TNI's role in containing religious, ethnic, or other localized conflicts are somewhat stronger, especially since the potential for communal violence seems likely to diminish in the medium term. The most prominent communal tension today is between Muslim and Christian communities, particularly in Sulawesi. Conflicts between fundamentalist and moderate Muslims could arise in the near

---

7. For each threat, the effectiveness of the government's strategy will depend critically on the intelligence function. For the organization and operation of intelligence activities, see issue 18.

term, and perhaps between indigenous groups and migrants from other parts of Indonesia in another generation or so.[8]

DOMESTIC TERRORISTS. The capacity of the National Police to find and apprehend terrorists has improved rapidly in recent years with the benefit of technical assistance and equipment from the United States, Australia, Japan, and other countries. However, the TNI remains closely involved, using concerns about terrorism as a reason to maintain and even strengthen the army's territorial command structure. Various historical and institutional factors as well as external pressures related to the U.S.-led war on international terrorism also make it difficult to reduce TNI's role.

ORGANIZATIONAL ISSUES. The division of labor between the TNI and National Police is hampered not only by functional issues but also by several critical organizational issues. First, the existing laws and regulations relating to defense and security are contradictory, overlapping, and incomplete. A robust defense and security regime will require a new set of mutually compatible laws and regulations.[9] A draft law on national (homeland) security under discussion in early 2007 would put the National Police under the Ministry of Home Affairs. However, the minister of defense has suggested putting the National Police under the Ministry of Defense in the interest of "maximizing the coordination and control of the national security and defense actors."[10] This idea drew strenuous objections from the head of the National Police, illustrating that positions on the basic approach to national defense and security are still far apart.

Second, in Indonesia's newly decentralized system of regional autonomy, the respective responsibilities of the regional/local governments and the National Police for maintaining public order remain uncertain.[11] Under Law 2 of 2002 on the Police, the only police force in the country is the National Police. While this structural choice has not been controversial, it can be viewed

8. The Mobile Brigade of the National Police is a highly trained quasi-military force that has been deployed against secessionists in Aceh and in areas of communal conflict. It has been linked to human rights abuses in the past but could be strengthened as an alternative to using TNI units to deal with major threats to public order.

9. The legal shortcomings in the defense and security sector are examined in detail in Sukma (2006). As many as seventeen draft laws related to this sector were being worked on at the beginning of 2007. Wisnu Dewabrata and M. Hernowo, "Upaya Menata Hubungan 'Saudara Tua-Muda,'" *Kompas*, January 16, 2007.

10. Press report from the Coordinating Ministry for Political, Legal, and Security Affairs, January 9, 2007. Some TNI supporters have argued that making the TNI commander responsible to the Ministry of Defense would require a constitutional amendment.

11. A number of cities have a small municipal police force (*polisi pamong praja*). Jakarta's police force has fewer than 700 members.

as somewhat inconsistent with Indonesia's democratic system and highly diverse society. One alternative would be to establish independent police forces in each region (*daerah*) to deal with local crimes and to restructure the National Police to focus on national crimes. Confusion in this area is compounded by the recent practice among regional governments of allocating funds from their budgets to both the TNI and the National Police.

ISSUE 12

What role will the TNI play in protecting natural and strategic resources?

As mentioned earlier, the unlicensed exploitation of its natural resources is the biggest external threat to Indonesia today, and it is an even larger threat internally. Hence the protection of Indonesia's natural resources depends not only on securing control of the country's borders but also on strengthening its ability to detect illegal activities by any party and to apprehend the perpetrators.[12]

Given the archipelagic nature of Indonesia's territory, the arguments are strong for assigning to the TNI the task of border surveillance as well as surveillance over the vast expanses of thinly populated land and ocean where natural resources are located. The technology for satellite surveillance has improved to the point where it may be highly cost-effective to depend primarily on this technology rather than airborne or sea-based surveillance.[13] Pilotless drones may be another low-cost means of conducting surveillance to detect illegal burning of forests or poaching of fish.[14] Assigning this task to the TNI would be efficient because of its technical expertise and experience. Fur-

---

12. Under the 1982 UN Convention on the Law of the Sea, the territorial waters of every maritime nation extend out 12 nautical miles from its coast. A "contiguous zone" extends out another 12 nautical miles. An "exclusive economic zone" extends out 200 nautical miles from the coast. Sovereign states have full jurisdiction over "internal waters," and all waters within the boundaries of an archipelagic nation are considered internal waters. *Wikipedia* (October 27, 2006).

13. The cost of building a surveillance satellite, putting it in orbit, and setting up tracking stations can be as low as $100 million. Dehqanzada and Florini (2000, p. 57).

14. A news report from www.suaramerdeka.com, posted on the TNI's history website (www.sejarahatni.mil.id) on October 18, 2006, disclosed TNI plans to purchase unmanned aerial vehicles from Israel using export credit funds from the 2004 budget. This procurement was to be made via a small Philippines-linked corporation doing business in food and other consumer nondurables.

thermore, enhancing the TNI's role in enforcement could boost discipline and discourage misconduct among all of the agencies concerned.

Although Indonesia established a special security regime in 2004 to protect its "strategic resources" or "vital national objects" (see chapter 4), there is still some uncertainty about the respective roles of the TNI and the National Police in protecting such objects. On one hand, it is difficult to reconcile this kind of guard duty with a fully professional TNI.[15] On the other hand, the National Police do not appear to have the capacity to provide all of the protection required.

ISSUE 13

What role will the TNI play in peacekeeping operations in other countries organized by the United Nations or other international bodies?

Between 1957 and 2003, Indonesian units participated in UN peacekeeping operations in eighteen countries.[16] The scope for greater participation is substantial, especially if the TNI is able to improve its image as a professional service committed to respecting human rights.

Indonesia can derive substantial benefits from such operations, perhaps the greatest being increased visibility for a country that is grossly underrepresented in world affairs given the size of its population. Other foreign policy benefits accrue from being seen as a reliable partner in contributing to "global public goods," reinforcing its role as a leader of the nonaligned movement and reminding people that democratic governance can thrive in a Muslim-majority country. Exposing midlevel TNI officers to the personnel and practices of other countries is an additional benefit, as President SBY himself can attest. Since UN peacekeeping operations often deal with ethnic violence, Indonesian participation can also provide opportunities to keep up with state-of-the-art techniques that may be applicable at home.

All of these benefits presumably outweighed the costs when the government decided in August 2006 to participate in the UN Interim Force in Lebanon (UNIFIL), despite public concerns about helping Israel in any man-

15. In a forum on June 20, 2006, Major General Dadi Susanto, director general for strategy in the Ministry of Defense, commented on the inconsistency, citing anger expressed to him on a recent trip to Papua by members of an airborne Kostrad battalion assigned to guard the Freeport-McMoRan installation.

16. Ministry of Defense White Paper (2003, pp. 62–63). The first UN operation in which the TNI participated was in Egypt. Altogether, the TNI has provided ninety-five armed units and military observer teams.

ner.[17] The Indonesian contingent, designated Garuda XXIII, includes personnel from all three services and is structured as a mechanized infantry battalion of roughly 900 soldiers and an engineering company of roughly 100 soldiers.[18]

Policy Issues Related to Implementing a National Defense and Security Strategy

Designing a credible defense and security strategy is just a first step in putting the TNI fully on budget. A number of crucial issues will then arise in the process of implementing the strategy. Six are examined in this section (for historical background, see appendix A).

ISSUE 14

How will the new TNI doctrine evolve?

In January 2007 the government announced a new military doctrine, titled TRIDEK. Its main thrust is recognizing the separation of the National Police. Further elaboration of TRIDEK, or its replacement, will presumably occur after a new national defense and security strategy is in place.

A number of countries today are placing greater emphasis on nonconventional military operations in their military doctrines. A case in point is the German government's decision of October 2006 to focus on international peacekeeping and thus undertake the most radical restructuring of its armed forces since 1945.[19] TRIDEK appears to be consistent with the broader trend in its emphasis on "non-war operations."[20]

17. The costs are significant. The United Nations reimburses each soldier participating in UNIFIL, regardless of national origin, roughly $1,000 a month. Some equipment costs are also reimbursed. Nonreimbursed costs related to equipping, moving, and supporting the Indonesian contingent for UNIFIL are being met by drawing on the general reserve fund in the central government's budget. DPR member, interview, December 21, 2006.

18. TNI Press Release, September 4, 2006 (www.tni.mil.id).

19. They will be transformed in stages into "international intervention forces" that will allow the deployment of 14,000 troops on five simultaneous missions out of a total strength of 250,000 troops. Hugh Williamson, "Germany's Military to Take on Global Role," *Financial Times*, October 25, 2006, p. 1.

20. Said (2006a, p. 287) argues for seeking a broad social consensus in formulating the doctrine of the TNI: "Our choice of defense doctrine is a matter too important to be left to the military alone because it must be remembered that the choice does not involve only technical military matters. The choice should be a political one made by the people via their representatives in the Parliament and the People's Consultative Assembly." TRIDEK appears to be a purely TNI product.

An important part of implementing TRIDEK will be to clarify the relationship between the TNI and the civilian authorities, particularly between the TNI commander and the minister of defense. Under Article 10 of the 1945 Constitution, the civilian president is the supreme commander of the army, navy, and air force. Law 3 of 2002 on National Defense empowers the president to appoint the TNI commander, with the approval of the House of Representatives. The commander is therefore responsible to the president for directing TNI forces and "works with the Minister in fulfilling the needs of the TNI." This arrangement has been criticized on the grounds that civilian control is best established by making the military commander responsible to a civilian minister of defense.[21]

Another important implementation issue concerns the role of the National Defense Council (Dewan Pertahanan Nasional, DPN), which has yet to be activated. Law 3 of 2002 provides for the creation of this body, to be chaired by the president and to include as permanent members the vice president, minister of defense, minister of home affairs, and the TNI commander. Its purpose is to advise the president on general defense policy and the mobilization of all national defense components. Its activation would also reinforce civilian control of the military.[22] With the National Defense Council in place and the TNI commander reporting to the minister of defense, ending the TNI's involvement in business activities and putting the TNI fully on budget might proceed more rapidly.

ISSUE 15

What will be the relative strength of the army, navy, and air force?

As pointed out by many military analysts inside and outside Indonesia, the army's dominance of the military establishment is inconsistent with the tangible threats to Indonesia's security and with the archipelagic character of the country (see chapter 3 and appendix A). In their view, the emphasis should shift toward the navy, accompanied by a significant strengthening of the air force.[23]

---

21. This issue is closely linked to the issue of the reporting responsibility of the head of the National Police. The TNI would be deeply offended if its commander were required to report to the Minister of Defense while the head of the National Police continued to report to the president. One option under consideration is to put the National Police under the Ministry of Home Affairs.

22. See discussion in Rizal Sukma (2006).

23. In an essay written before his appointment as minister of defense, Juwono Sudarsono sketched out a framework showing budget allocations to the army, navy, air force, and police at 33:19:13:35 in 2004 and 30:25:15:30 in 2012. USINDO (2004, p. 28).

The army's resistance to a shift of this kind is easy to understand and is bolstered by two arguments related to existing budget constraints. First, any such reduction in a country where unemployment may be the biggest single political issue looks like a recipe for trouble. Second, the cost of equipping, training, and maintaining navy and air force units tends to be substantially higher than for army units.

Without a national defense strategy as a basis for determining the desired force structure, it is difficult to know how far and how fast to implement these structural adjustments. As a benchmark, a 10 percent reduction in the budget for the army would be equivalent to a 28 percent increase in the budget for the navy or a 36 percent boost for the air force.[24] A shift of this magnitude would be out of the question within one fiscal year but might be feasible if stretched out over three to five years.

ISSUE 16

What will be the role of other forces that can bear some of the burden of internal security?

Three forces merit consideration in this context: local militias, a military reserve, and a coast guard.

LOCAL MILITIAS. Indonesia has a host of militias linked to various organizations, including political parties and religious groups. The nomenclature of the government-sponsored groups alone is daunting. Hansip, short for Pertahanan Sipil (Civil Defense), had as many as five million members nationwide at the turn of the new century. In addition to being called upon to maintain public order and help deal with natural disasters, they provide income relief for the unemployed.[25] The Ministry of Home Affairs is responsible for Hansip, which includes at least three distinct forces organized at the village level that are supported and mobilized by other authorities. The Wanra (People's Resistance Organization) was created by the TNI for the purpose of waging "people's warfare" against a foreign invader. The Kamra (People's Security Organization) was created by the National Police (its members get about three weeks of basic training each year).[26] Linmas (Community Pro-

---

24. Based on the program allocations in the central government's budget for 2007, which earmarked Rp 13.5 trillion for the army, Rp 4.9 trillion for the navy, and Rp 3.7 trillion for the air force. See chap. 8, table 8-5.

25. International Crisis Group (2001a, pp. 6–7).

26. Sebastian (2006, pp. 476–77).

tection) units are created by local governments.[27] While there may be arguments for dissolving the Wanra and the Kamra as the National Police become better able to maintain internal security, they do perform useful social functions, are not a significant drain on budget resources, and do not create economic distortions.

Over the past fifty years, more than a dozen private militias have been supported by the TNI, by mass movements such as Muhammadiyah and Nahdlatul Ulama, and by others. Most have been co-opted by the government, but a few significant ones remain active and autonomous.[28] With the strengthening of the National Police, the arguments for terminating the private militias will look more attractive.

One policy option for government-sponsored militias would be to upgrade the operational capacities of the Hansip components without changing the basic structure. Another option would be to merge the militias into a military reserve force (see the next section). Alternatively, some of these components could be replaced or supplemented with a "national guard" force along the lines of the National Guard in the United States.[29]

A MILITARY RESERVE. Article 8 of Law 3 of 2002 on National Defense provides for a reserve component consisting of "citizens, manufactured and natural resources, and the national facilities and infrastructure prepared for mobilization." Article 60 of Law 34 of 2004 on the TNI also provides for activating discharged soldiers in the event of a military emergency or war. In practice, Indonesia does not have a meaningful reserve force, but early in 2007 the Ministry of Defense was at work on a law creating one.[30]

Historically, the authorities in Jakarta (including the TNI) have resisted the creation of a military reserve for fear that reserve units in some regions might join separatist forces. This cannot be a serious concern today given the sweep-

27. Other bodies with a security role are the Municipal Police (*pamong praja*), the Siskamling (Neighborhood Security System), and guard services licensed by the National Police known as *SATPAM*.

28. Sebastian (2006, pp. 476–77).

29. In a potentially significant step in this direction, the Hawaii National Guard has initiated a "State Partnership Program" with Indonesia, due to be formally inaugurated in the first half of 2007 on the occasion of a visit to Jakarta by the governor of Hawaii and the commander of the Hawaii National Guard. Information from an officer in the National Guard Bureau, January 23, 2007.

30. In 2003 the reserve units of eight regional army commands consisted of 900 members. Roughly 25,000 university students were receiving basic training in university regiments, and graduates of these regiments totaled 60,000 or more. Government of Indonesia, Ministry of Defense (2003, p. 70).

ing decentralization of authority from Jakarta in 2001. One of the great attractions of a military reserve is that it would cost less to have a substantial number of well-trained military personnel on part-time rather than full-time salaries.

A COAST GUARD. Article 6 of Law 2 of 2002 assigns the National Police responsibility for law enforcement in the "whole territory" of Indonesia, which implicitly includes the sea as well as the land within Indonesia's borders. At the same time, Article 9 of Law 34 of 2004 on the TNI tasks the navy to "uphold the law and safeguard the security in our maritime territory of national jurisdiction."

In practice, law enforcement in Indonesia's territorial waters is a shared responsibility of seven government agencies: the Indonesian Navy, the Marine Police (*polisi perairan,* within the National Police), the Sea and Coast Guard Unit (KPLP) and the National Search and Rescue Agency (within the Ministry of Transportation), the Surveillance and Control of Marine and Fish Resources Office (within the Ministry of Marine Affairs and Fisheries), the Customs Service (within the Finance Ministry), and the Immigration Office (within the Ministry of Justice and Human Rights). Even when combined, these forces lack the capacity to enforce laws in more than a small fraction of Indonesia's waters.[31] While the division of responsibilities among the seven agencies is not always clear, the Marine Police bear the heaviest burden of enforcement.[32] This agency also represents Indonesia in meetings with coast guard forces from other countries.[33]

Various proposals for improving maritime security were under debate at the beginning of 2007. These included a proposal to create a full-fledged coast guard under the Ministry of Transportation.[34] Foreign experts have advocated an independent coast guard agency for Indonesia, but the advantages of doing so are debatable. If resources for maritime security continue to be severely constrained, then incremental improvements in the enforcement capacities of the Marine Police and the navy, along with an evolving division of responsibilities, may be the best course. However, substantial commitments

31. In 2005 the coordinating minister for political, legal, and security affairs established a Security Coordinating Body to improve relations among the five agencies, but its effectiveness remains to be demonstrated. Prodita Sabarini, "Coastline Vulnerable to Smuggling," *Jakarta Post,* September 6, 2006.

32. The Marine Police has 5,870 members spread out over thirty-one National Police districts. *Indosiar News Report,* August 4, 2006 (www.indosiar.com).

33. The second meeting for heads of coast guard agencies in Asia was held in Malaysia in March 2006, hosted by the director general of the Malaysian Maritime Enforcement Agency (http://webevents.bernama.com/events/mmea2006/head.php [October 2, 2006]).

34. Andi Widjajanto, interview, December 20, 2006.

of foreign aid could alleviate the budget constraints, in which case creating an independent coast guard could have the advantage of starting fresh and escaping some of the cultural baggage of the past.[35]

Will the army's territorial command structure be replaced or modified?

The Army's territorial command structure (described in appendix A) appears to be more extensive than any similar structure elsewhere in the world. It is deeply rooted in Indonesia's postindependence experience and is one of the most controversial subjects of military reform today. Without question, the territorial command structure provides opportunities and incentives for business activities that would not exist if the army had a more conventional structure of operational divisions, brigades, and battalions.[36]

The territorial command structure up to 1965 was a legacy of the country's fight for independence. In the Suharto era, this structure was maintained superficially for the defense of the nation via the doctrine of people's warfare, but more fundamentally for the perpetuation of a patronage-based political system.

As seems clear from the nature of external and internal threats (see issue 8), the strongest argument for maintaining the territorial command structure in today's democratic political system is to help the National Police in maintaining public order throughout the archipelago (including combating terrorism). However, there is no compelling rationale for keeping such a structure beyond the next five to ten years.[37] In particular, it does not appear to be essential for the defense of the nation. Other force structures can be equally or more effective for that purpose.[38]

35. The United States is providing substantial assistance to the Marine Police as part of its program to strengthen the National Police.

36. "Because economically Indonesia is not yet able to fund all the needs of its army, *Koter* [Territorial Command] plays an important role in covering the shortfall in funding experienced by the military at the institutional level but especially at the individual level.... The use of the territorial commands to augment funding for institutions or individuals is an important factor in understanding the frequent clashes between the Indonesian Army and the Indonesian Police since the reformation." Salim Said (2006a, pp. 250–51).

37. M. Asfar, in UNSFIR (2005), examines in detail four reasons for giving up the territorial command structure. He describes at length the main alternatives that have been considered since the adoption of the TNI's New Paradigm.

38. Citing an interview in 2002, Sebastian concludes: "In all likelihood, all territorial functions from the Kodim level below could be abolished without diminishing the fighting capacity of the TNI at the regional level." Sebastian (2006, p. 212).

A leading military reformer, Lieutenant General (retired) Agus Widjojo, who served as chief of the army's Territorial Staff from 1999 to 2002, identified two alternatives to the existing territorial command structure: retract its reach to the village level or replace it with an army simply organized around operational divisions. Under the former option, the existing units at the district (*kabupaten*), subdistrict (*kecamatan*), and village (*kelurahan*) level—Kodim, Koramil, and Babinsa, respectively—would be reassembled at the provincial (Kodam) level and moved to bases outside the provincial capitals to reinforce the nonpolitical nature of their missions.[39] A variation on this theme is to remove the top three layers—Kodam, Korem, and Kodim—and leave the lowest two layers.

A third alternative is to organize the TNI into three Regional Defense Commands (Kowilhan, Komando Wilayah Pertahanan), each one responsible for roughly a third of Indonesia's territory, with army, navy, and air force units integrated under a single command for each region.[40] This alternative has been studied by the TNI for the past five years but has no prominent champions at the present time.

A fourth alternative is to create five Area Defense Commands (Kodahan, Komando Daerah Pertahanan),.[41] Unlike the Kodam commanders who control only army units, each Kodahan commander would command an integrated force of army, navy, and air force units. All of the army's organic battle battalions under the current territorial command structure would be reorganized into five divisions modeled on Kostrad's structure. The five Kodahan would be oriented toward the main sea lanes passing through the archipelago.

In the course of this study, we were unable to find any estimates of the cost of moving to a new force structure. However, our inquiries did suggest, first, that any cost savings from moving away from the territorial command structure are likely to be small. Second, substantial additional budget funds would be required to make Indonesia's existing force structure fully operational (by repairing idle equipment and filling gaps). Third, foreign assistance to facilitate the restructuring of the TNI could have a major impact on the ultimate shape of the force and the pace at which it can be overhauled.

It should be understood that restructuring is not an all-or-nothing proposition. For example, an experimental structure could be introduced within three years in one specific region and then adapted in phases to other regions,

39. Salim Said (2006a, pp. 287–88).
40. Sebastian (2006, pp. 209–15).
41. Andi Widjajanto and Edy Prasetyono (2006, pp. 26–31).

on the basis of the initial experience. Or the new structure could be introduced in a skeletal fashion and then fleshed out over five to ten years. The cost components are clear: land acquisition for new bases, new buildings (especially for integrated command staff), weapons and equipment, physical relocation of personnel and units, and some new hiring (especially for the navy and air force). [42]

ISSUE 18

How will intelligence activities be organized, how should official secrets (classified information) be protected, and what information should the public have access to?

The domestic intelligence function has passed through many incarnations since independence, though always dominated by the TNI's intelligence capability, which is linked to the army's territorial command structure. In the Suharto era, the extent of surveillance and operational activities of the TNI intelligence apparatus was on a par with those of other highly centralized authoritarian regimes. Not surprisingly, Indonesian intelligence personnel were implicated in some of the worst human rights abuses of the Suharto era.

In the Reformasi era, the civilian governments have taken various steps to dilute the TNI's role in domestic security, the most notable being to split off the National Police in 1999. At the beginning of 2007, however, the TNI's role in domestic intelligence remained strong and not fully under the control of the civilian authorities.[43] A major concern here is that much of the TNI's domestic intelligence activity is funded by off-budget revenue.[44]

As 2007 began, work was under way on a draft law on intelligence and a related law on official secrets. These are important aspects of military reform, but they fall outside the scope of this study. A new law on official secrets, in combination with one on freedom of information currently under discussion, could put additional pressure on the TNI to disclose more information about its business activities.

---

42. The TNI probably has sufficient land already to meet most requirements under a new structure. Furthermore, it controls a large amount of high-value land in and around Jakarta that is not well located for defense purposes and could be sold to fund much if not all of the new requirements.

43. One option under consideration is to split the State Intelligence Agency (Badan Intelijen Negara, BIN) into separate agencies for domestic and foreign intelligence. R. B. Hubir, "No Matter Who's the Boss, BIN in Need of Reform," *Jakarta Post*, February 7, 2007.

44. American military expert, interview, November 26, 2006.

ISSUE 19

Will a new military justice law provide effective disincentives for the TNI to continue engaging in business activities?

Since the Reformasi period began, TNI officers have been steadily withdrawing from visible business positions. This trend was reinforced by the passage of Law 34 of 2004 on the TNI, which contains a provision (Article 39) forbidding soldiers to become involved in business activities. However, no specific penalties are prescribed for violating this provision. Article 62 provides for discharging soldiers without honor "because of his/her character and/or deed which truly damaged military service discipline or TNI," but at this stage it could be hard to show that any business activity did significant damage. Another problem is that the regulations required to implement Article 62 had not been issued as of the beginning of 2007.

A related concern is the TNI's culture of impunity. Though under assault, it remains intact. In 2006, in response to public complaints, the government initiated work on a new military justice law.[45] If a strong law emerges and is enforced visibly and promptly, it could provide a substantial incentive for TNI personnel to discontinue off-budget revenue-generating activities. In other countries such as South Korea, headline-producing examples that the culture of impunity was coming to an end were key signals that civilian supremacy over the military had been achieved.[46]

---

45. The passage of the draft law was held up by a debate over the implementation of Article 65 in Law 34 of 2004, which provides for the prosecution in civil courts of soldiers who have been accused of committing civil crimes.

46. Salim Said (2006a, pp. 195–28).

8

Budget Realities

> Possession of modern sophisticated equipment does not necessarily lead to
> victory. And that is because every single force, anywhere in the world, is con-
> structed in accordance with a purpose: a defense and security policy and a
> military doctrine, which demands certain amounts of troops and materials of
> specific qualifications, that all interlock into a coherent force. . . . [L]ack of
> coherence—whether in purpose or between purpose and force—is a major
> reason for the failure of forces. Beyond geography, money has always been the
> greatest deciding factor in the structure of a force.
> —Rupert Smith, *The Utility of Force*

After developing a credible defense and security strategy, a major
challenge for the Indonesian government will be ensuring that the military
budget is large enough to implement the chosen strategy. To find a feasible
path to this end, the government will have to resolve various issues related
to the budget, including their impact on "the welfare of soldiers."

The Military Budget

As a share of the central government's budget and in relation to GDP, the
defense budget dropped sharply in the 1970s, fell further during the 1980s,
held steady at a lower level through the 1990s until Suharto resigned in 1998,
and has fluctuated around an even lower level since then (table 8-1). Furthermore, when Indonesia's military expenditures are compared with those of
its most important neighbors, not only in terms of dollar value but also in
relation to population size, GDP, and land area (table 8-2), Indonesia appears
to be spending substantially less than its neighbors.

Table 8-1. *The Defense Budget as a Share of the Central Government Budget and in Relation to GDP, 1970–2005*

Percent

Defense	1970	1975	1980	1985	1990	1995	2000	2005
As share of central government budget	23.5	16.9	11.3	10.6	7.0	7.7	4.3	5.6
In relation to GDP	n.a.	3.6	2.9	2.5	1.5	1.6	1.0	1.0

Source: Widjaja in UNSFIR (2005), unnumbered appendix table.
n.a. = Not available.

The figures cited in table 8-2 should be approached with a degree of caution, however. First, military expenditures as defined by the Stockholm International Peace Research Institute (SIPRI) cannot be equated with the defense budgets of the countries listed. Second, it is not clear that expenditures, especially those off the budget, are comparable. Third, converting local currency expenditures into dollar values using current exchange rates muddies the comparison. Fourth, the land area figures for Indonesia and the

Table 8-2. *Military Expenditures and Share of GDP in Six Countries and How They Compare by Number of Armed Forces Personnel, Population, and Land Area*

Country and number of armed forces personnel, 2003	Population (million)	Land area (square miles)	Military expenditures[a] (billions of U.S. dollars) 1999	2002
Indonesia, 302,000	246	1.8 million[b]	1.649 (0.9)	2.774 (1.1)
Philippines, 106,000	90	300,000	0.719 (1.1)	0.763 (0.9)
Thailand, 314,000	65	510,000	1.907 (1.6)	1.808 (1.2)
Malaysia, 104,000	24	330,000	1.762 (2.1)	2.703 (2.3)
Australia, 54,000	20	7.6 million	8.606 (1.9)	10.214 (1.9)
Singapore, 73,000	4	690	4.481 (5.4)	4.814 (4.7)

Sources: Bonn International Center for Defense Conversion for armed forces personnel (via SIPRI First Database); Central Intelligence Agency, *World Factbook, 2006*, for population and land area; SIPRI First Database for expenditures (in 2003 U.S. dollars and exchange rates) and share of GDP.
a. Figures in parentheses indicate percent of GDP.
b. Indonesia's archipelagic waters cover six million square miles of ocean. Sebastian (2006, p. 240).

Table 8-3. *Central Government Budget for 2007*
Trillions of rupiah

Accounts	Amount
Discretionary, by agency	
Education	43.5
Defense[a]	31.3
Public Works	21.4
National Police[a]	18.7
Health	15.6
Religious Affairs	10.8
Aceh-Nias Reconstruction	10.0
Transportation	9.5
Agriculture	8.2
Finance	7.7
Foreign Affairs	5.4
Energy and Mineral Resources	4.5
Maritime and Fisheries	3.0
60 other agencies	46.7
Total discretionary	234.0
Nondiscretionary	
Debt service	85.1
Subsidies	141.3
Other	35.4
Total nondiscretionary	261.8
Total budget	496.0

Source: Government of Indonesia, Ministry of Finance, 2007 Budget Statistics, table 7.
a. Defense and National Police figures represent the total budget for defense and security.

Philippines, both archipelago nations, substantially understate the amount of territory these countries are responsible for defending and securing.

In 2007 the defense budget totaled Rp 31.3 trillion ($3.4 billion), which accounted for 13 percent of the discretionary portion and 6.3 percent of the total budget, giving it the second largest share after education (table 8-3). The budget for the National Police was the fourth largest, at Rp 18.7 trillion ($2.0 billion). Thus the overall defense and security budget was substantially larger than the education budget. A breakdown of the defense budget by expense category (personnel, goods and services, capital equipment) and by service (table 8-4) clearly shows that the army dominates the military forces, and that personnel costs account for 45 percent of the total defense outlay in 2007.

Table 8-5 provides a breakdown of military personnel by rank and service, while table 8-6 shows the base salary scale for the military, per month, from second private to major general. When added together, allowances can be

Table 8-4. *Defense Budget for 2006 and 2007*
Billions of rupiah

Item	Total 2006	Total 2007	Personnel	Goods and services	Capital equipment
TNI Headquarters	3,388	4,184	650	2,897	637
Army	10,929	13,315	10,373	1,961	1,181
Navy	4,319	4,937	2,277	1,248	1,412
Air Force	3,344	3,681	1,144	1,224	1,312
Ministry of Defense	6,248	6,323	197	729	5,396
Local currency (own funds)ᵃ	1,798	2,102	197	729	1,176
Foreign currency (export credit)ᵃ	4,450	4,221	0	0	4,221
Total	28,229	32,640ᵇ	14,641	8,060	9,939

Source: Government of Indonesia, Ministry of Defense. Undated table provided to the authors on December 13, 2006.

a. "Local currency" and "Foreign currency" represent procurement of equipment, especially weapons. The local currency portion is funded by internally generated tax revenue. The foreign currency portion is funded by export credit agencies in the United States and other foreign countries.

b. The total for 2007 is different from the amount in table 8-3 because it reflects a small amount added by the parliament in the process of approving the government's budget.

larger than base salaries. There are also automatic deductions for retirement, health care, and other items. Base salaries are low by almost any standard. A private getting Rp 793,000 ($85) a month cannot support himself alone, especially in a high-cost region such as Jakarta. A brigadier general earning Rp 1.6 million ($171) a month is going to have trouble paying university fees for just one child.

Table 8-5. *Breakdown of Defense Personnel by Rank and Service, 2006*
Number of personnel

Personnel	Ministry of Defense	TNI Headquarters	Army	Navy	Air Force	Total
Senior officers	59	95	94	107	79	434
Middle officers	442	1,025	6,545	2,387	1,458	11,857
Junior officers	125	1,090	19,900	6,131	5,767	33,013
Noncommissioned officers	260	2,828	113,274	24,636	12,061	153,059
Soldiers	88	1,963	135,358	24,564	8,142	170,115
Total TNI	974	7,001	275,171	57,825	27,507	368,478
Civilian employees	4,335	4,935	46,204	8,502	5,353	69,329
Total defense	5,309	11,936	321,375	66,327	32,860	437,807

Source: Government of Indonesia, Ministry of Defense. Undated table provided to the authors on December 13, 2006.

Table 8-6. *Military Pay Scale, 2006*
Monthly base salary, thousands of rupiah

Rank	Lowest	Highest
General	2,276	2,515
Lieutenant General	2,207	2,436
Major General	1,591	2,362
Brigadier General	1,543	2,291
Colonel	1,496	2,221
Lieutenant Colonel	1,461	2,184
Major	1,407	2,089
Captain	1,364	2,025
1st Lieutenant	1,323	1,964
2nd Lieutenant	1,283	1,881
Chief Warrant Officer	1,169	1,652
Warrant Officer	1,134	1,602
Sergeant Major	1,099	1,554
Chief Sergeant	1,066	1,506
1st Sergeant	1,034	1,461
2nd Sergeant	1,002	1,416
Chief Corporal	925	1,244
1st Corporal	897	1,207
2nd Corporal	870	1,170
Chief Private	843	1,134
1st Private	818	1,100
2nd Private	793	1,067

Source: Government of Indonesia, Ministry of Finance. Directorate General of the Treasury, Surat Edaran No. SE-03/PB/2007 tentang Penyesuaian Besaran Gaji Pokok Pegewai Negeri Sipil . . . Anggota Tentara Nasional Indonesia. . . , January 15, 2007.

The "core" figures in official budget documents do not fully reflect the budget resources available to the TNI in any one year.[1] Other sources include: (a) supplemental budgets regularly approved by the House of Representatives (DPR) midway through the fiscal year; (b) transfers from the president's budget, usually from the "contingencies" line item; (c) transfers from the budget of the State Secretariat for special operations, such as security for a summit meeting of the Association of Southeast Asian Nations; (d) transfers from the budgets of regional authorities, which are funded in large part by central government revenues shared with the regions; (e) unspent funds from

1. It is important to distinguish the budget as approved by the DPR from the budget proposed by the government. In recent years, the difference has been small at the aggregate level. Most reporting and analysis are based on the budget proposal.

previous fiscal years; (f) service fees; and (g) discounts from market prices, special access, and payment arrears.

Summing up the constraints on the defense budget, military analyst Andi Widjajanto notes that voters favor butter in the classic "guns-versus-butter" trade-off, and because threats are fairly low, the government itself gives low priority to defense. Furthermore, the government's ability to raise revenue through taxation remains weak, it still has not produced a credible strategic defense plan, and the procurement of arms and equipment is plagued with corruption.[2] Our examination of the defense budget raises some additional points:

—No serious study of the defense budget exists at the present time. The government has the expertise to produce such a study—in its Supreme Audit Board (BPK), the Ministry of Finance, the National Development Planning Board (Bappenas), and the Ministry of Defense—but the staffs of these agencies are stretched thin working on other more important budget issues (such as fuel subsidies). Outside the government, Indonesia's think tanks, universities, and nongovernmental organizations do not appear to have the expertise required and may not for at least the next five years.

—As documented by the BPK and others, budget management is weak throughout the government and in the Ministry of Defense in particular. Leakages, diversion, and misreporting are the most notable problems. However, some improvements are taking place.

—Indonesia apparently has never had a "zero-based" defense budget driven by objectives with the total built up from a clean slate, without regard to past expenditures. The general pattern has been to increase the previous year's budget incrementally to compensate for inflation and accommodate minor program changes.

—The Ministry of Defense and the TNI are feeling little pressure from the public or the DPR to improve budget management. The main source of pressure at present seems to be the Ministry of Finance.

—There is little evidence of civilian supremacy in the preparation of the defense budget, which seems to be driven more by TNI Headquarters than by the Ministry of Defense or any other government agency.

Policy Issues Related to Major Budget Parameters

In mid-2006, Defense Minister Juwono Sudarsono pointed out that "since the mid-1950s, no Indonesian government has been able to provide the police

2. "Evaluasi Anggaran Pertahanan Indonesia," *Sinar Harapan*, June 25, 2005.

and defense force with an adequate budget."[3] Many experts within and out-side Indonesia would agree, although they might differ in their definition of an adequate budget. As already mentioned, the military budget is a relatively small fraction of the central government budget. Its future growth and com-position will depend on how the government addresses the policy issues outlined in the following sections.

How rapidly will the government allow the military budget to grow over the next five to ten years?

Over the next five years, the central budget is likely to grow faster than gross domestic product (GDP) because the country's tax revenues relative to GDP are low by international standards and have been rising at a brisk pace in response to improved policies and administration. Although the govern-ment has been aiming for 7–8 percent real GDP growth a year, the rate has not exceeded 6 percent in any year since the Reformasi era began in 1998. Central government spending has increased 10–15 percent a year in real terms even as the budget deficit has been shrinking. Subsidies (especially for fuel) are the biggest component of the budget, 28 percent in 2007, and reducing these further would provide room for a more rapid increase in discretionary spend-ing. If GDP continues to grow at an average annual rate of 6 percent up to 2012, central government spending can be reasonably expected to grow at 12–15 percent annually in real terms. These assumptions are consistent with the medium-term fiscal framework (2006–10) prepared by the World Bank for the June 2006 meeting of the Consultative Group on Indonesia (see the first line of table 8-7, which projects central government spending *before* adjusting for inflation).[4]

In the central government's budget for 2007, Rp 31.3 trillion ($3.4 bil-lion), or 6.3 percent of total spending of Rp 496 trillion ($53 billion), has been allocated for defense. As a base case, we assume that the defense share of the budget will remain constant at 6.3 percent to 2012. We have also calculated a "slow-growth path," with defense share rising to 6.9 percent in 2009 and 7.8 percent in 2012, and a "rapid-growth path," with defense share rising to 7.7 percent in 2009 and 9.8 percent in 2012 (see table 8-7). In the absence of a national defense and security strategy, however, it is impossible to say whether either benchmark would be adequate. So much depends on other policy

---

3. Sudarsono, "Indonesian Military and Rights," *Jakarta Post*, June 28, 2006, p. 6.
4. World Bank (2006, p. 11).

Table 8-7. *The Defense Budget Projected to 2012*[a]

Billions of rupiah

Projected item	2007	2008	2009	2012
Total central government spending	496.0	563.0	639.0	934.2
Defense share, base case	31.3	35.6	40.2	58.8
	(6.3)	(6.3)	(6.3)	(6.3)
Slow-growth path	31.3	37.2	44.1	72.9
	(6.3)	(6.6)	(6.9)	(7.8)
Fast-growth path	31.3	39.4	49.2	91.6
	(6.3)	(7.0)	(7.7)	(9.8)

a. Figures in parentheses represent percent of total spending.

choices examined in this chapter, such as reform of the social insurance system for the civil service generally.

According to the Ministry of Defense, the minimum funding requirement consistent with its current responsibilities and force structure would come to Rp 74.5 trillion ($8.0 billion), compared with the Rp 31.3 trillion ($3.4 billion) it was given.[5] By this measure, assuming the TNI's requirements do not change appreciably over the next five years, the allocation in 2012 would be 22 percent below the minimum requirement in the base case. Under our calculated slow-growth path, the allocation in 2012 would come very close to meeting the minimum requirement, and it would do so a year sooner on the high-growth path.

Without a great deal more information on what the TNI is doing with its existing budget allocation, and what it would do with the budget increases that seem politically feasible in the next five years (base case), the arguments for allocating a larger share of the budget to defense are not compelling. By the 2009 deadline for ending off-budget funding, the defense budget would grow by Rp 9 trillion ($1.0 billion) under the base case and by Rp 18 trillion ($1.9 billion) under the fast-growth case. Both of these figures are orders of magnitude above the amount of off-budget revenue that we estimated to be available to the TNI for operational purposes in 2006, which was Rp 408 billion to Rp 872 billion ($42 million to $91 million) (see chapter 5).

ISSUE 21

To what extent will regional (*daerah*) governments be permitted to provide financial and other support to the military?

5. Document given to the authors by the Ministry of Defense on December 13, 2006.

Given the way the territorial command structure has become embedded in the fabric of Indonesian society, it is not surprising that regional governments started funding local commands after the decentralization of authority in 2001. No systemic analysis of these payments appears to exist, but anecdotal evidence suggests that they are widespread and substantial. Such a review is clearly in order as a step toward establishing rules on what this funding can be used for and how it should be reflected in the TNI's budget and toward mitigating potential conflicts of interest.

ISSUE 22

To what extent will the efficiency of the military budget increase?

According to conventional wisdom, central government ministries and agencies have been misappropriating or wasting as much as 30 percent of their funds (by paying more than the market price or procuring goods that are not used for their intended purpose). There is no reason to believe that the rate of "leakage" in the military has been any lower than in the civilian agencies. The rate of leakage may drop below 30 percent in 2007 as a result of recent reforms, but it will undoubtedly still be significant. A drop in the leakage rate of 5 percentage points would free up an additional Rp 1.6 trillion ($170 million) that could be used to raise military salaries or procure new equipment.

The rate of leakage in the military is unlikely to shrink substantially as long as it remains high in the civilian agencies. However, the military could conceivably be a "first mover" in this area and provide a model for the rest of the government. Whether the TNI could be persuaded to assume this role would depend on the military leadership, military doctrine, and behavioral incentives.

A core challenge in reducing leakage lies in addressing procurement problems, which the press has featured since the beginning of the Reformasi era.[6] Although many of the alleged abuses are based on unsubstantiated information, one example may be enough to illustrate the complexities involved. The TNI's annual budget includes an amount for gas and other fuels to be purchased from Pertamina. In recent years the TNI has spent substantially more

6. *Tempo* Magazine ran a series of reports on military spending problems in its April 18–24, 2006, issue (no. 33/6). One story concluded with the following thought: "The TNI could become a pioneer in the fight against corruption if it were able to [set] a good example by cleaning up its own act. TNI discipline should not be restricted to marching in line and following orders. It should also extend to the use of state funds."

on fuel than assumed in its budget, accumulating arrears to Pertamina on the order of Rp 1.9 trillion ($200 million) at the end of 2005.[7] It is not clear whether the excess was related to increased fuel consumption or higher prices, but it represents a hidden form of off-budget funding.

Another efficiency challenge lies in the trade-off between spending for maintenance and spare parts and spending for new equipment. The fastest and most efficient route to greater operational readiness is to spend more on maintenance and to purchase spare parts for worn-out and damaged equipment. The tendency in the past, however, has been to procure new equipment instead.

ISSUE 23

How much military equipment will be procured from the domestic defense industry?

Indonesia's defense industry emerged during the revolution and grew slowly over the next three decades. It expanded more rapidly in the 1980s under Suharto's protégé, Habibie, who fathered a network of companies as part of an ambitious plan for a technology-based defense industry. The companies were hard hit by the financial crisis of 1997–98, and during his brief tenure as president Habibie could do little to revive them. They suffered further neglect under Presidents Wahid and Megawati.

Although Indonesia has the technical capacity to expand the defense industry, demand from the TNI is now weak. Financing to expand the industry could come from procurement orders (foreign as well as domestic), the government budget, or the banking system, but these sources are limited. In the context of this study, the trade-off between foreign and domestic procurement is particularly interesting. Domestic procurement creates jobs and helps to keep Indonesia's foreign debt service burden within reasonable bounds. On the other hand, superior-quality military hardware can be obtained from foreign suppliers at highly competitive prices, and often with highly favorable financing terms.

Most of Indonesia's indigenous defense industry is in the public sector, dominated by five state-owned enterprises nominally under the direction of the Ministry of State-Owned Enterprises. The largest of the five is P.T. Dirgantara Indonesia, the conglomerate created by Habibie in 1976, previously

---

7. Finance Ministry official, interview, July 3, 2006. The amount budgeted for fuel in 2005 was Rp 800 billion ($100 million).

known as IPTN, which has been manufacturing helicopters and small planes under license for many years.[8]

Because state-owned enterprises have a history of poor performance, a case can be made for privatizing some or all of them. However, corporate governance in Indonesia has also been weak. In the medium term, it may be more prudent to seek incremental improvements in each company and defer privatization until management teams can deliver a sustainable solid performance and thereby provide the basis for a leveraged buyout.

Another means of strengthening the defense industry, discussed at a ministerial meeting in January 2007, would be to reduce Indonesia's dependence on foreign suppliers by reallocating some of the present foreign currency funding to domestic procurement.[9] However, such a move may reflect politically driven economic nationalism more than a desire to increase budget efficiency.

ISSUE 24

How much foreign aid will the military be allowed to receive?

In the Reformasi era, foreign military assistance (on grant, concessional loan, or export credit terms) has been constrained by the objective of reducing Indonesia's external debt burden and by foreign concerns about the military's past behavior. After the terrorist attacks of September 11, 2001, in the United States and the subsequent attacks in Indonesia, military assistance started increasing again, with a sharp upturn after President Susilo Bambang Yudhoyono (SBY) took office in 2004 and the U.S. Congress lifted its restrictions on military aid to Indonesia at the end of 2005.[10]

In the period ahead, as long as the military appears to be moving toward civilian control and more professional behavior, the trend in foreign military assistance is likely to remain upward, constrained by the government's reluc-

8. For more information on P.T. Dirgantara Indonesia, see www.indonesian-aerospace.com/history. The other four companies are P.T. Pindad (small arms and munitions), P.T. PAL (shipbuilding), P.T. Dahana (explosives), and P.T. LEN Industri (electronics and communications). Sebastian (2006, pp. 254–55). Most of these companies manufacture goods for the private sector as well as the TNI.

9. "Government Plans to Do Its Arms Shopping at Home," *Jakarta Post*, January 11, 2007. In the same report: "'We will make efforts to encourage strategic industries and private firms to work together to develop a domestic defense industry,' Juwono was quoted by Detik.com as saying. However, Juwono said the government was not aiming for the development of a heavy armaments industry, but was rather focusing on the development of a mid-level one."

10. Among a number of important training initiatives under way, the United Kingdom is supporting an eighteen-month degree program in defense management.

tance to assume additional nonconcessional debt. Two other factors will be critical: the military's choice of foreign suppliers and suppliers' conditions related to internal TNI reforms. The military's past preference for U.S. equipment may be waning in the face of strong competition from other suppliers, notably Russia, China, and India. As announced in November 2006, Indonesia has already agreed to purchase $1 billion of Russian weapon systems (including fighter jets, assault helicopters, submarines) over the next five years.[11] If Indonesia decides to restructure its forces, foreign aid might also be available to fund a substantial portion of the cost of equipping new bases and new operational units.

ISSUE 25

How will the government's policy change regarding off-budget financing for the military?

With the transfer of TNI business activities to the government by 2009 pursuant to Article 76 of Law 34 of 2004, the net income from those activities will theoretically flow to the central government instead of the military, and then the same amount will be allocated to the TNI's budget. Thus the TNI would end up with the same resources as it had before, except that now they would all come from the budget. The theory breaks down over three practical difficulties, however: it may take years to untangle the government's stake in individual business units and resolve the claims of other parties in the courts; the liabilities of many TNI businesses may be greater than their assets, meaning they are bankrupt and need to be auctioned off or closed down; and the net income of these businesses may drop sharply after being transferred to the government because they no longer enjoy the patronage or protection of the TNI.

In the interest of putting the TNI fully on budget, a more reasonable approach is to assume that the net income from the TNI's business activities in the future will be zero and not to rely on this source of funds to meet any of the TNI's operational requirements. Our finding that the amount of this net income is relatively small underscores the wisdom of this approach. If the TNI is able and prepared at some point to disclose specific streams of off-budget revenue that should be replaced by budget resources, then the zero assumption can be changed.

11. Agence France-Presse, November 17, 2006.

Policy Issues Related to Soldier Welfare

The passionate and often repeated rationale for the TNI's business activities is that they provide for the welfare of the soldiers. This argument can be challenged on four counts. First, more efficient use of current budget resources could yield significant improvements in welfare for low-ranking soldiers. Second, the amount of off-budget funds actually used to this end appears to be quite small. Third, the TNI could increase compensation and related benefits and reduce equipment and other nonpersonnel costs, although this would further impair its operational readiness. Fourth, the number of military personnel could be cut back, perhaps by as much as one-fifth, without adversely affecting the country's defense and security by a measurable amount. The main obstacle to changing the compensation structure (base salary, allowances, and benefits) for the military is that it is tightly linked to civil service compensation.

ISSUE 26

How will the structure of civil service salaries evolve and will the military salary structure continue to be linked to it?

Civil service salaries in Indonesia have been depressed for decades, owing to the traditional pressures of patronage and the fear of aggravating unemployment if civil service positions are eliminated. With base salaries too low even to support minimal standards of living, civil servants in virtually every central and local government body are engaged in moonlighting, the diversion of nonsalary budget funds, and myriad rent-seeking activities.

Note, however, that base salaries alone do not accurately reflect civil service and TNI/National Police compensation. For one thing, as grade levels rise, civil servants gain access to special allowances (for example, for travel), project payments (for example, for project management or attending meetings), or in-kind benefits (such as a car). Second, those allowances add up to substantial amounts.[12] Thus at the level of an office director, base salaries typically

---

12. Allowances recently included: (1) spouse allowance, equivalent to 10 percent of base salary; (2) child allowance, equivalent to 3 percent of base salary for up to two children under the age of eighteen or in school; (3) rice allowance, in cash for up to four family members; (4) structural allowance, for employees with managerial responsibilities; (5) functional allowance, for employees with professional skills such as doctors; (6) housing allowance, a one-time grant for relocating; (7) external pay, for employees posted overseas; (8) overtime; and (9) honoraria, for project implementation. Nunberg and others (2000).

represent less than one-half of total compensation.[13] Hence, as pointed out in a recent World Bank report, overall compensation is not as poor as generally assumed:

> Though civil service base salaries are low relative to private sector and international benchmarks, the overall compensation package is characterized by a wide range of allowances and honoraria many of which are non-transparent, discretionary and highly prone to abuse. Once the total compensation package is considered, studies show that many segments of Indonesia's civil service have *not* [emphasis added] been systematically underpaid compared to workers in the private sector. The problem . . . may not be the level of pay, but the opaque and discretionary system for determining overall compensation and its weak link to either personal or group performance.[14]

Fortunately, the SBY government is committed to reforming the civil service and raising salaries—as demonstrated by the 20 percent increase in its compensation budget for 2006 and the 23 percent increase for 2007. More fundamentally, according to the World Bank, the government is developing a new remuneration policy for the most senior officials (*pejabat negara*), the Finance Ministry and the Education Ministry are working on compensation initiatives that could become models for broader reforms, and the legal framework for the civil service is being updated.[15]

Since independence, military salaries have been directly linked to civil service salaries, with the base salary of a private matching the lowest level on the civil service pay scale.[16] Precedents exist for de-linking civil service and military pay scales. For example, the pay scale for central bank employees has for years been substantially higher. The pay scale for employees of the Indonesian Bank Restructuring Agency (IBRA) was higher during its existence from 1998 to 2004, and the pay scale for employees of the Aceh reconstruction agency (BRR) was higher when it was established in 2005. Both of these are temporary agen-

13. A comprehensive assessment of civil service/TNI compensation must also take into consideration the compulsory deductions for pensions, health care, and other benefits, most of which are substandard due to flawed funding mechanisms.

14. World Bank (2006, p. 47). See also Steadman and Kendall (2005).

15. World Bank (2006, pp. 47–48).

16. One form of allowance is provided exclusively to TNI personnel: *uang lauk pauk*. This is a daily allowance for food that has its roots in the revolution. It has been raised to Rp 30,000 for 2007, adding up to Rp 900,000 ($97) a month, equivalent to the base salary of a first corporal. TNI personnel also receive allowances—for participation in operations away from their base, for serving in special positions, and for accepting specific duties—that are equivalent to the special allowances provided to civil servants.

cies and both were designed to handle exceptionally large amounts of money, which justified their generous compensation structure. The military has guns, however, which could also justify an elevated compensation structure.

The elements of a grand bargain in this area are present. With a credible commitment by the TNI to end its business activities, a new doctrine more consistent with a professional military, and a new defense and security strategy based on smaller and more mobile operational units, for example, a case could be made for putting the military on a higher pay scale than the civil service.[17]

Another option would be to move a substantial number of military personnel from full-time to part-time status to better conform with the current reality, which finds many soldiers not engaged in meaningful activities on a full-time basis and almost all having second jobs. A third option would be to convert military personnel currently engaged primarily in bureaucratic tasks to civil service staff and make it the core of a reserve force that could be mobilized in emergencies. A fourth option would be to introduce a location allowance for high-priced locations such as Jakarta and sharply reduce the number of military units located in the Jakarta region.

ISSUE 27

What provisions will be made for military personnel pensions?

The first pension law after independence was passed in 1956 and replaced by a second law in 1969.[18] Curiously, the agencies created to implement the pension system were in the form of profit-making state-owned enterprises, initially as P. N. (*Perusahaan Negara*, State Enterprise) and subsequently as P. T. (*Perseroan Terbatas*, Limited Liability Corporation) entities. The enterprise responsible for civil servant pensions, P. T. Taspen, was founded in 1963; a separate one for military and police personnel, P. T. Asabri, was founded in 1971. A third company, P. T. Jamsostek, was formed to run a pension plan for private sector companies, and a fourth, P. T. Askes, was formed to manage health insurance plans for both the public sector and the private sector.

In 1998, at the end of the Suharto period, Indonesia's social insurance system was in disarray. Coverage was thin and unreliable. Misuse of funds was commonplace. Transparency and accountability were minimal. The burden

17. While there are crucial differences between the TNI and the People's Liberation Army (PLA), this is more or less the deal the government of China made with the PLA in 1998. Between 1978 and 1998, China reduced the size of its armed forces by half. Chua Chin Hon, "Message of Peace from the Guest," *Straits Times*, September 3, 2005, p. 7.

18. Rachmatarwata (2004, p. 2).

on the budget was substantial and growing. Years of work on a new national social insurance system, encompassing military and police personnel, civil servants, and private sector workers, eventually bore fruit with the passage of Law 40 of 2004. The new law is bitter fruit, however. It contains serious flaws and not much of it has been implemented in the two years that have elapsed since it was signed.[19] Thus the old system continues to limp along.

The TNI, the National Police, and the civilians employed by these agencies still make mandatory monthly contributions to P. T. Asabri. These contributions amount to 4.75 percent of base-salary-plus-allowances for pensions, and 3.25 percent for a "social insurance" package of four benefits: (a) a savings benefit—provident fund—"for old age and housing" paid upon retirement to defense personnel eligible to receive a pension; (b) a cash value benefit paid to personnel discharged honorably before reaching retirement age; (c) a death benefit of Rp 35 million ($3,800) paid to survivors of personnel who die before retirement or are killed on duty; and (d) burial costs paid for all active and retired personnel when they die.[20]

The retirement age for military and police officers is fifty-eight years, compared with fifty-five years for civil servants.[21] The pension benefit is 2.5 percent of the final year's base salary and family allowances for each year of service up to a maximum of 75 percent. Pension contributions are deducted from taxable income; pensions themselves are fully taxed. For the most part, pension payments from Asabri are reliable, but Asabri's accumulated surplus is small and shrinking rapidly. The gap between contributions and payouts is covered by the budget, and the new law seems more likely to aggravate this burden than alleviate it.[22] Despite the gap, P. T. Asabri pays dividends and taxes to the government.

P. T. Asabri's management of the savings plan is scandalous. Participants are given little information about the status of their accounts. The lump-sum payments due on retirement are unpredictable and seem to be discretionary. In a recent and typical incident, the military police allegedly loaned Rp 226

19. Arifianto (2004, pp. ii–iv).

20. On social insurance for the Indonesian Armed Forces, see *Peraturan Pemerintah*, no. 67, 1991.

21. The retirement age for ordinary soldiers is fifty-three. The unusual policy of setting a higher retirement age for military personnel originated in Law 34 of 2004 on the TNI (art. 53).

22. In a late 2003 report, the World Bank wrote: "All pension funds have suffered from lack of transparency and disclosure, weak management information systems and internal corporate governance, and directed investments under political influence." As the report also noted, the Asian Development Bank estimated the cash flow deficits of P. T. Taspen and P. T. Asabri in 2000 to be Rp 13.5 trillion ($1.5 billion) and Rp 30 billion ($3.4 million), respectively. World Bank (2003b, p. 25).

billion ($24 million) of Asabri funds to a businessman to build a housing complex, but the houses were not built and the businessman only returned a portion of the money.[23]

One policy option would be to keep the TNI on a separate pension system and transform P. T. Asabri into a model for implementing a broader civil servant pension reform. The obstacles to making this option work are formidable, however. Asabri seems to be the least efficient and transparent of the state-owned social insurance corporations. Thus the only realistic option may be to wait for the government to begin implementing the 2004 law, which envisions merging Asabri and its sister corporations into a new nonprofit government agency. The difficulty here will be reconciling the ambitious objectives of the 2004 law with the budget constraints Indonesia is likely to face over the next five or more years.

ISSUE 28

What provisions will be made for military personnel housing benefits?

Housing is a major issue for the military. On-base housing is rarely available for more than half of the TNI personnel assigned to a particular base. Junior soldiers tend to live in barracks on base while more senior ones live off base. By contrast, senior officers tend to have access to decent and free housing on base, while junior officers scramble for off-base housing. Clearly, some of the income from military business that is spent for the welfare of soldiers (as distinct from the amounts used for operational or other purposes) goes for housing. Substantial amounts of both on-base and off-base housing have been built with funding from military foundations and cooperatives.

P. T. Asabri is an important source of funding for housing. After serving for a number of years, soldiers are allowed to withdraw funds from their compulsory savings accounts to make down payments on houses.[24]

---

23. "Kasus dana perumahan prajurit dilimpahkan ke polisi militer," *Tempo Interaktif,* August 1, 2006.

24. The housing fund for civil servants (Dana Perumahan) is no better and perhaps worse. According to a recent International Monetary Fund report: "The housing fund [for civil servants, Dana Perumahan], created in 1993, is entirely off-budget and not recorded in government accounts. The fund is financed by compulsory monthly salary deductions from civil servants, which can be used for a down payment on house purchases or renovations or can be withdrawn as a lump sum (without interest). Its policy status is unclear; while it could be interpreted as a social security scheme, it is not reported as such. The government is currently deciding on the housing fund's future." IMF (2006, p. 6).

Another institution involved in housing is the Foundation for Soldiers' Housing (*Yayasan Kesejahteraan Perumahan Prajurit*, YKPP), established by the Ministry of Defense, which also provides soldiers with funds for down payments on houses. In addition, each of the services has a housing program for its personnel. The Ministry of Defense is now studying the possibility of combining the separate programs into one, in the form of a state-owned enterprise with professional management and high performance standards.[25] The wisdom of this approach as opposed to a more private sector–oriented approach is questionable.

If it is assumed that half of all TNI personnel, roughly 180,000 people, are without adequate housing and the cost of building a decent house averages Rp 50 million to Rp 70 million ($5,400 to $7,500), then the cost of providing new housing for TNI personnel living in substandard conditions would be about Rp 9.7 trillion to Rp 13.5 trillion ($1.4 billion to $1.5 billion), or 30–40 percent of the defense budget for 2007. If this cost were stretched out over five years, the impact on the budget would be commensurately smaller and perhaps politically feasible.

In short, providing substantially better housing for the TNI does not look like a budget buster. Moreover, there are less burdensome ways to finance housing construction. For example, commercial banks could provide the necessary financing with support from a government guarantee program.

ISSUE 29

What provisions will be made for the health and education of military personnel and their families?

Several issues merit attention in these areas of military compensation.

HEALTH. In addition to the 4.75 percent deduction for their pensions and the 3.25 percent deduction for their "social insurance" package, all defense personnel contribute 2 percent of their basic pay for health services. The health care they receive for this contribution depends on their branch of service and the location of their posting. In principle, all defense personnel and their families are eligible to receive free medical care from military-owned/controlled hospitals and on-base clinics. However, many military personnel do not have easy access to good hospitals, doctors, and related medical services.

Military hospitals provide some generic drugs, but most drugs have to be purchased from pharmacies in the private sector. Because military salaries are

25. Ministry of Defense news item, March 10, 2006 (www.dmc.dephan.go.id).

often too small to allow soldiers to bear the market price of medicines, unit commanders commonly draw on discretionary funds, including funds in related foundations and cooperatives, to assist soldiers in purchasing medicine.

A useful step toward improving benefits in this area would be for the Ministry of Defense to commission a study of the current amount of off-budget spending for health services and the options for either privatizing these health services or putting them on budget. A critical part of such a study would be to focus on the military-controlled hospitals, most of which are owned by military foundations.[26]

EDUCATION. Indonesia requires children to attend school up to the age of thirteen. Although there are no formal tuition charges in public schools through the third grade, other charges and "contributions" are common and can represent a serious burden for low-ranking soldiers. Here, also, unit commanders often draw on discretionary funds to assist soldiers in meeting these costs. Their ability to do so varies greatly from unit to unit, depending on how "wet" or "dry" it is. Here again, a useful step would be to commission a study of off-budget expenditures and options for privatizing the educational institutions under the TNI's control.[27]

ISSUE 30

What benefits will be made available to disabled soldiers and their widows and orphans?

Defense ministry officials and TNI leaders frequently cite the inadequate funding for disabled soldiers and widows/orphans as a reason for engaging in revenue-generating activities. As noted earlier, medical care for soldiers is free in principle, but apparently the cost of modern prosthetics is not covered by the Asabri benefit or the budget. Consequently, unit commanders have turned to foundations and cooperatives for money to procure suitable prosthetics for disabled members of their units. The costs involved cannot be large. It may not be difficult, therefore, for the government to adopt a policy on prosthetics and other disability benefits, and to include a specific line item in the budget to cover this cost.

Widows/widowers/orphans receive survivor benefits when a defense employee dies in service (see issue 27). However, the amount is not considered

26. The leading TNI hospital is Gatot Subroto Central Army Hospital in Jakarta, which has its origins in a hospital founded by the Dutch colonial administration in 1819. It was turned over to the Indonesian Army in 1950.

27. One of the best known of these institutions is the navy's Hang Tuah University in Surabaya, which is owned by the navy's foundation.

sufficient to support a minimum standard of living. Consequently, unit commanders have been using discretionary resources from foundations and cooperatives to help widows/widowers/orphans live a decent life. Again, the total cost cannot be large. Thus the use of discretionary funds could be eliminated by adopting a policy of providing more generous support and allocating budget funds specifically for this purpose.

This is yet another area in which a study of on-budget and off-budget spending would be a useful next step. Improving benefits for defense personnel will, of course, have implications for the provision of the corresponding benefits for civil servants. A case can be made, however, for granting more favorable treatment to defense personnel on the basis of the hazards of their occupation.

PART III

The Way Forward

9 | Observations and Implications

Our intention in this study has been to avoid recommending specific policies for winding down the business activities of Tentara Nasional Indonesia (TNI) en route to full budget funding. Instead, we have concentrated on the essential background information required to identify alternative policies, analyze the implications of these alternatives, and make sensible policy choices.

We adopted this approach for three reasons. First, the process of putting the TNI fully on budget is complex and involves parts of the government beyond the Ministry of Defense and the TNI. At the present time, the government's desire to undertake reforms in this area outstrips its ability to implement meaningful changes. Moreover, responsible officials are still uncertain about the approach to be taken and the pace at which to proceed.

Second, some powerful groups have a vested interest in concealing detailed, auditable information about the sources and uses of the TNI's off-budget income. Without such details, an objective assessment of how the TNI's current operations are funded is not possible.

Third, since the beginning of Reformasi, many sensible proposals have been advanced for "modernizing" the Indonesian Armed Forces, but few of them have been adopted. What Indonesia would benefit from now is a stronger political and social consensus on the need to change old patterns of behavior, not more ideas about what or how to change.

Nevertheless, to provide a greater sense of closure for this study, we offer a few observations for the Indonesian government, the Ministry of Defense, the

TNI, and foreign donors. For the Indonesian government generally, progress in the following six areas will make the goal of putting the TNI fully on budget much easier to reach. Without progress in these areas, it will be impossible to do so by 2009, the government's current deadline, and maybe not for another ten to twenty years.

—*Restructuring and raising civil service compensation to make it less discretionary and more closely linked to performance.* De-linking military compensation from civil service compensation and putting it on a faster reform path is a potentially attractive alternative.

—*Sharply improving the financial management of the pension system, the health insurance system, and the compulsory savings system (and its link to housing finance) for public sector employees.* Moving the military into its own health system might be an improvement, but only if accompanied by a major advance in the administrative efficiency of the military bureaucracy. More generally, the challenge is either to make the new national social insurance system work or to revise it so that it will perform at a satisfactory level.

—*Improving public sector transparency and fiscal accountability across the board.* Off-budget funds, diversion of budget funds, and other budget-related shortcomings are not unique to the TNI. Progress elsewhere in the government will make it easier to improve transparency and accountability in the defense sector. Transferring military businesses to the government will yield few benefits as long as enterprises already in the government's portfolio continue to obstruct growth more than drive it.

—*Developing a policy on public sector foundations that is consistent with modern standards of good governance.* An obvious first step is to increase the transparency of all public sector foundations promptly. A commitment to close down most of them within five to ten years would help to change the image of the government from that of a privileged and self-serving elite to an instrument for achieving a just and prosperous society.

—*Developing a policy on the non-tax revenues of government ministries and agencies that come from the rental or leasing of state assets, primarily land and buildings.* Putting these revenues on budget is likely to be easier than ending the TNI's reliance on income from illegal activities.

For the Ministry of Defense and the TNI, progress in five areas would help to demonstrate their commitment to becoming a world-class professional military establishment. The benefits of doing so could include increased public support domestically and increased foreign assistance to strengthen the operational capacities of the army, navy, and air force.

—Producing a credible strategic plan for national defense and security. To be credible, the plan will have to be more than a wish list and more than a justification of the status quo. Modifying the army's existing territorial command structure could contribute a substantial measure of credibility.

—Becoming a model for budget transparency. In many countries, the defense budget is one of the least transparent components of the state budget. Building on its tradition of national leadership, the military could gain significant benefits from becoming a pacesetter in this area.

—Taking visible and early steps to demonstrate that the TNI is exiting from its formal business activities. A strategy of doing nothing is attractive because the value of the TNI's formal businesses may easily shrink to nothing within three years without any effort on the part of the government, but it would reinforce the impression that the TNI is trying to maintain its independence from the government. Transferring one or two TNI businesses to the Ministry of State-Owned Enterprises without waiting for a new agency to be created could help to show that the TNI's new doctrine of TRIDEK is a major step forward.

—Developing a road map for full budget funding. It is hard to imagine any plan that would achieve this objective by 2009. Full budget funding by 2012 may be feasible, however, by building on work that Bappenas, the National Development Planning Board, has done.

—Initiating studies in areas where the obstacles to reform are fewer or the benefits of reform are larger. The promising areas we singled out include security services, commercialization of state assets, transfers from regional governments, health and education support, and support for disabled soldiers, widows, and orphans. Studies focusing on the TNI foundations and cooperatives would require more substantial efforts.

Foreign countries and international institutions interested in helping the TNI move on budget could also have a large positive impact on the pace of progress. Their input could consist of both technical and financial assistance.

—Technical assistance to upgrade the planning and budgeting, administrative, and operational capacities of the Ministry of Defense and the TNI. By improving their ability to evaluate alternative technologies, these agencies could be in a better position to produce a credible national defense and security strategy. With advice on best practices in preparing budgets, the TNI might be less anxious about making the defense budget transparent. Adopting more open and competitive procurement procedures, the TNI could gain increased respect both inside and outside the country. With help in training newly restructured units, the military could greatly increase its operational readiness.

—*Financial assistance to help the TNI obtain the most appropriate foreign equipment on the most favorable terms.* In addition to ensuring that military procurement does not become a debt burden, foreign financing can help to ensure that scarce resources are not wasted on nonessential or obsolete weapons systems and equipment.

A Brief History of the TNI and Its Current Structure

For readers who are not familiar with Indonesia or the TNI, the information in this appendix is intended to provide additional background relevant to our study.

The Role of the TNI in Indonesia's History

The role of the TNI has evolved through distinct phases associated with the war for independence, the constitution of 1950, internal warfare, guided democracy, the "new order," and Reformasi.

The War for Independence (1945–49)

Days after Japan surrendered to end World War II in August 1945, Sukarno and other leaders of the nationalist movement declared Indonesia's independence. In short order, the provisional government dissolved the self-defense force on Java and Bali created by the Japanese as an instrument of occupation (Tentara Peta), the people's militia on Sumatra (Laskar Rakyat), and the Indonesian auxiliaries attached to regular Japanese army units (Heiho). These forces were formally replaced by the Tentara Nasional Indonesia (TNI) on October 5, 1945, in a decree signed by President Sukarno.[1]

In the very first month of independence, the armed forces were placed under a civilian authority that evolved into the Ministry of Defense. Even so, the TNI was more of a "self-created" entity than a product of the civilian government.

---

1. This account of TNI history is drawn largely from Widjojo, Widjajanto, and Sigit (2005, pp. 12–23).

The core of the early TNI consisted of a young generation of student fighters (Tentara Pelajar).[2] To this were added various autonomous militia units, the most important being the People's Security Corps (Badan Keamanan Rakyat, BKR). Former Indonesian members of the Dutch colonial army, KNIL, were also a vital source of talent.[3]

The TNI's initial defense strategy against the Dutch was a "Maginot Line" concept, with "own" territory on one side and "enemy" territory on the other, but it quickly gave way to the use of "defense circles" in the face of overwhelming Dutch firepower. In 1946, the doctrine enunciated by TNI Commander Sudirman evolved into a classic guerrilla warfare posture, in which locally supported units harassed their superior enemy opportunistically throughout the contested area. Refined again in 1947 as a "Total People's Defense," it now included all elements of civil society in the struggle for independence. The force that evolved to implement this doctrine was the "territorial command" of the army, consisting of units mirroring the administrative structure of the civilian government, from the provincial level to the village level. This structure, and the TNI's organization into divisions, brigades, and regiments, was formalized in Law 3 of 1948.[4]

Constitution of the United States of Indonesia (1949–50)

In October 1949, the Dutch agreed to recognize the Indonesian government based on a new constitution (the 1950 Constitution) that created the United States of Indonesia. Within a year, however, the individual states in the federal structure dissolved and merged into the unitary Republic of Indonesia.[5]

Internal Warfare (1950–59)

During the 1950s, several military operations were organized to crush serious regional rebellions, notably in West Java, Aceh, other provinces on Sumatra, and South Sulawesi. The operation against the Darul Islam rebellion in West Java followed a strategy of encirclement (Pagar Betis) that combined concepts of territorial warfare and people's defense. The operation against the PRRI/Permesta rebellion adopted a more or less conventional strategy of surprise attacks using combined land, air, and sea forces.

2. Said (2006a, p. 37).

3. Samego and others (1998, pp. 45–47).

4. During its occupation of Indonesia, Japan introduced the concept of organizing the population at the neighborhood and village level. This experience was a factor in the design of the army's territorial command structure. Sebastian (2006, pp. 277–78).

5. Said (2006a, p. 9).

The operations to suppress regional rebellions did not change the basic doctrine of People's Defense, which was reaffirmed in Law 29 of 1954. This law also maintained the TNI as an instrument of the government.

The parliamentary form of government established under the Constitution of 1950 was not a success. It was marked by extreme factionalism and a high degree of instability. Policy uncertainty became a major impediment to economic growth, and the euphoria that had accompanied independence steadily dissipated. Sukarno's vision of leadership also turned increasingly outward during this period, especially after the hugely successful summit of leaders from the "nonaligned nations" in Bandung in 1955. His anticolonial, anti-imperialist rhetoric soared to new heights as he sought to spread Indonesia's revolution to other oppressed people around the world.

"Guided Democracy" (1959–67)

Constitutional democracy was put in the deep freeze in March 1957, when martial law was declared. In December 1957, Dutch businesses were nationalized, with military officers put in charge of many of them. In July 1959 Sukarno reinstated the Constitution of 1945 by decree and over the next six years struggled to maintain control as his country became increasingly divided between the left, represented by the Indonesian Communist Party (PKI); the right, represented by several Muslim parties; and the nationalist middle, favored by the military.[6]

At the end of 1961, having failed to persuade the United Nations to force the Dutch to relinquish control over West Irian (the western half of the island of New Guinea), Sukarno declared Indonesia's intention to liberate the territory. A joint command was formed under General Suharto to achieve this objective. Suharto adopted a conventional three-year strategy beginning with infiltration, followed by open attack and occupation, and finishing with consolidation. To support this campaign, reserves were mobilized, more than 60 percent of the government's budget was allocated to the military, and a large number of weapons were purchased from the Soviet Union and its Eastern European satellites. International pressure bore fruit in August 1962 when the Dutch agreed to turn West Irian over to the United Nations on October 1, with a further transfer to Indonesia on May 1, 1963, following a referendum.

While the referendum was questionable in its execution, Indonesia gained possession of West Irian in May 1963 without any further military action. As the campaign for West Irian wound down, however, Indonesia entered into a

---

6. An excellent analysis of the military's first twenty years can be found in McVey (1971, 1972).

"confrontation" with Malaysia in response to the formation of a new nation from the British colonial territories on the Malay Peninsula and the island of Borneo (now Kalimantan). The campaign against Malaysia was a rallying point for the PKI, but it was a military flop. It also precipitated Indonesia's decision to walk out of the United Nations in January 1965 when Malaysia was seated. The campaign continued until September 30, 1965, arguably the most fateful day in Indonesia's history.

An aborted military coup on that date undermined Sukarno's leadership. Stability was restored by General Suharto, initially from his position as commander of the army's strategic reserves (Kostrad). It took Suharto more than two years to consolidate his power. In March 1967 the People's Consultative Assembly (MPR) stripped Sukarno of all his titles and appointed Suharto the new president. A year later, the MPR elected Suharto to a full five-year term as president.

Several other developments during this period are noteworthy:

—In 1957 Indonesian military units participated for the first time in a UN peacekeeping operation (in Egypt).

—In November 1958 army commander A. H. Nasution delivered a speech proposing the TNI should adopt the "Middle Way," functioning as neither the dominant source of power nor simply the tool of the civilian government. This was the beginning of the doctrine of Dwifungsi (dual functions), which called on the TNI to play a leading role in the political and economic life of the country. Several historians have noted that Dwifungsi was inspired in part by officers trained in the United States who were exposed to academic arguments that the military was a natural leader of modernizing forces in developing countries.[7]

—In 1959 Sukarno began to push the concept of "functional groups" (*golongan karya*) as counterweights or alternatives to political parties, which were seen as increasingly dysfunctional, with the TNI as the most important functional group.[8]

7. Said (2006a, p. 121). Note that democratic civilian rule was one of the premises on which the United Nations and the other international institutions were established at the end of World War II. As the cold war intensified, however, the United States and other Western democracies became increasingly enamored of military regimes in developing countries, which were seen as natural allies in the struggle against communism. A seminar sponsored by the Rand Corporation in 1959, subsequently documented in a book published by John J. Johnson (*The Role of the Military in Underdeveloped Countries*), was a seminal event in this shift. A generation of Indonesian military officers was exposed to the views emerging from this seminar in the training programs they attended at Fort Leavenworth and other military training centers in the United States in the 1960s and 1970s. Said (2006a, p. 121).

8. Said (2006b, pp. 15–16).

—In January 1962 the separate army, navy, air force, and National Police services were combined into the Indonesian Armed Forces (ABRI). The ABRI title was dropped in 1999 when the National Police became a separate force and the other three services reinstated the TNI title.

The "New Order" (1967–98)

Strong images of the TNI as the "pillar of the state" and the "savior of the nation" became firmly embedded in Indonesia's political psyche during the period of Suharto's rule. A good example is the following statement by Major General Ali Murtopo, a member of the small circle of personal assistants (Aspri, Assisten Pribadi) to Suharto:[9]

> From the history of our country we can conclude that it is only because of the presence of ABRI that the disintegration heading toward the destruction of our country several times could be avoided. Historically speaking ABRI is the only group in society which was born together with the new institution, namely the state based on *Pancasila*. . . . It is because ABRI has the ability and tradition to overcome group ideologies and interests that make[s] it the leader of the country.

With the exception of the annexation of East Timor in 1975, military operations during President Suharto's "New Order" regime were strictly internal and were dominated by the early post-coup campaign to exterminate the Communist Party and its supporters. A new overarching doctrine of Tri Ubaya Shakti (three sacred truths) emerged from a seminar at the Army Command and Staff School (Seskoad) in August 1966. Tri Ubaya Shakti combined the three basic doctrines of Pertahan Darat Nasional (Hanratnas, National Land Defense), Kekaryaan (Civilian Secondment), and Pembinaan (Guidance).

The doctrine of Hanratnas was basically defensive, designed as a last resort in the face of external attacks, and with the four goals of ensuring the nation's independence, sovereignty, and territorial integrity, safeguarding the national philosophy of Pancasila, and giving material and spiritual support for the development of the nation.

The Seskoad seminar was followed a month later by a Ministry of Defense seminar where the doctrine of Catur Darma Eka Karma (four duties one purpose) was adopted to reinforce Tri Ubaya Shakti. The four strategic "duties" of Catur Darma Eka Karma were operationalized in the form of seven elements, each of which was supported by a military command established under

9. Said (2006a, p. 24).

a presidential decree issued in 1967. Over the next sixteen years, the seven commands were reduced in stages to three commands. In 1974 one new command was also created that became closely identified with maintaining the Suharto regime and removing its enemies: Komando Operasi Pemulihan Keamanan dan Ketertiban, or Kopkamtib (Operational Command for the Restoration of Security and Order).

The concept of mobilizing the entire nation when under attack was further developed and reflected in Law 20 of 1982 on the Main Determinants of the Defense and Security of the Republic of Indonesia. This law spelled out the Sistem Pertahanan Keamanan Rakyat Semesta, or Sishankamrata (Whole People's System of Defense and Security). The law called for "arming the people mentally with the *Pancasila* ideology and physically with the capacity to defend the nation as directed by the government." In 1988 ABRI commander L. B. Moerdani issued an order reaffirming Catur Darma Eka Karma (CADEK) as the fighting doctrine of the military. This order called for Sishankamrata to be developed to "mobilize effectively all of the nation's resources and infrastructure in a manner that is total, integrated, and directed."

While it was General Nasution who introduced the doctrine of Dwifungsi, it was General Suharto who ten years later gave it operational meaning. At the same time, the primacy of the TNI as an institution implicit in Dwifungsi was more form than substance. The TNI became essentially an instrument of Suharto's personal rule.[10]

During the New Order period, military operations were conducted entirely within the country except in the struggle over the Portuguese half of the small island of Timor in the mid-1970s.[11] Following the end of António de Oliveira Salazar's authoritarian rule, the new democratic government of Portugal cut loose the country's miserably managed colonies in 1974. Conflicts broke out in most of these colonies between different internal factions. In East Timor, the Fretilin faction declared independence in November 1975. Two weeks later, the capital of East Timor (Dili) was captured in a clumsy operation by Indonesian forces. In July 1976 East Timor formally became a province of Indonesia.

Over the next fifteen years, Fretilin continued to fight for independence, despite successive TNI operations to crush the movement. Commercial exploitation of East Timor resources by the TNI and by Suharto's family and friends contributed to the growing pro-independence sentiment of this period.

10. Said (2006a, p. 274).
11. This account of the events in East Timor is drawn largely from Friend (2003).

East Timor captured global attention in October 1991 when TNI soldiers fired into a crowd of civilians gathered at the Santa Cruz cemetery for the burial of a pro-independence youth. The incident led to cutbacks in aid by a number of countries, including the United States. It also was instrumental in the Nobel Committee's decision to award the 1996 Peace Prize to Carlos Filipe Ximenes Belo, the Catholic bishop of East Timor, and José Ramos-Horta, the international spokesman for the independence movement.[12]

Reformasi (1998–)

From the end of the Suharto regime in 1998 until January 2007, the staff of the Ministry of Defense and the TNI relied on the doctrine of CADEK, with two major informal modifications: the basic domestic security function was transferred to the National Police (following its separation from the TNI in 1999), and the military abandoned its sociopolitical role.

On January 25, 2007, TNI's commander, Air Chief Marshal Djoko Suyanto, unveiled a new military doctrine titled Tri Dharma Eka Putra (three missions one deed), shortened to TRIDEK. It formally prohibited military personnel from involvement in "sociopolitical affairs," understood to include business activities as well as electoral politics. Equally important, it narrowed the doctrine to exclude the National Police, to reflect the separation of the police from the TNI in 1999.

Under TRIDEK, the principal task of the TNI is to "maintain the sovereignty of the nation, defend the territorial integrity of the Unitary State of the Republic of Indonesia (NKRI), and protect all the people and the motherland against all threats and interferences."[13] Furthermore, the TNI will implement TRIDEK through six specific "war operations" (such as land, sea, air) and fourteen "operations other than war." The non-war operations include overcoming separatist movements, combating terrorism, securing borders, supporting government at the regional level, assisting the National Police, assisting in recovery from natural disasters, and helping maintain maritime and air space security.[14]

---

12. The tragedy of 1991 was compounded by a two-week rampage by TNI soldiers and TNI-controlled militia forces in 1999 following a referendum in which 78 percent of the East Timorese voted against remaining within Indonesia with special autonomy. A UN peacekeeping force restored order, and East Timor became an independent nation in May 2002.

13. TNI headquarters press release, January 25, 2007.

14. A senior TNI official noted that normally a new doctrine follows the issuance of a new national defense strategy, but in this case the doctrine has come first. Emmy Kuswandari, "Doktrin baru jamin TNI tidak berpolitik," *Sinar Harapan*, January 25, 2007.

The Current Structure of the TNI

The TNI currently consists of three main forces: the army, the navy, and air force.[15]

Army

The army is divided between "territorial" and "central" forces. The territorial forces are structured to mirror the administrative divisions of the civilian government, but not in a strict fashion. For example, several Kodam cover more than one province, and the Babinsa covers more than one village. Together the territorial forces comprise 150,000 soldiers, roughly half of the army's strength. Among the territorial forces, 76,000 soldiers are assigned to infantry, cavalry, artillery, air defense, and engineering battalions. The rest are essentially bureaucrats, assigned to desk jobs related primarily to maintaining internal security. More detail is provided in table A-1.

The central forces consist of the Army Strategic Reserves (Kostrad), the Army Special Forces (Kopassus), and several TNI Headquarters units.[16]

—Kostrad has 27,000 personnel divided into two infantry divisions and an independent airborne brigade, based in Jakarta, Bandung (West Java), and Malang (East Java).

—Kopassus has about 3,500 personnel, based primarily in Jakarta. It consists of three headquarters groups, four covert warfare battalions, and one antiterrorist detachment.

—TNI Headquarters units include two aviation squadrons and two engineer construction battalions.

Navy

Navy headquarters is located in Jakarta. Operationally, the navy is divided between an Eastern Fleet and a Western Fleet. The marines, reporting to the navy commander, were reorganized in 2001 into the First Marine Corps Group, with about 6,500 personnel based in Surabaya, and the Independent Marine Corps Brigade, with about 3,500 personnel based in Jakarta.[17]

15. A recent and detailed discussion of Indonesia's force structure can be found in Sebastian (2006, pp. 233–49).
16. From Lowry (1996, pp. 229–40). No more recent breakdown appears to have been made public by the Ministry of Defense or the TNI Headquarters.
17. Sebastian (2006, p. 239).

Table A-1. *The Army's Territorial Command Structure*

Civil administration	Territorial command	Number of units
Province (*propinsi*)	Kodam	12
(No current equivalent)	Korem	39
District (*kabupaten*)	Kodim	271
Subdistrict (*kecamatan*)	Koramil	3,818
Village (*kelurahan*)	Babinsa	27,000–30,000

Sources: Lowry (1996, pp. 229–30); Yunanto and others, in Nurhasim (2005, p. 68).

Air Force

Air force headquarters is located in Jakarta. The air force includes fifteen operational squadrons, three training squadrons, and six ground defense squadrons. These units are assigned to seven air bases: Halim (Jakarta), Abdulrachman Saleh (Malang, East Java), Iswahyudi (Madiun, Central Java), Hasanuddin (Ujung Pandang, South Sulawesi), Atang Sanjaya (Bogor, West Java), Suryadi Suryadarma (Subang, West Java), and Pekan Baru (Sumatra).

Weapons Operability and Procurement

A fundamental weakness of the TNI is the extremely poor and obsolete condition of its weapons and equipment. By most accounts, more than 50 percent of the aircraft and major naval vessels in the inventory are inoperable, mostly because of the lack of spare parts.

The TNI procures much of its military equipment from foreign sources. Figures for the 1999–2003 period are shown in table A-2 but do not accurately reflect the sources of foreign-supplied equipment in the TNI's inventory. Historically, the TNI has had a strong preference for American weaponry. The breakdown by country of origin in 2004 was estimated to be 34 percent United States, 12 percent France, 12 percent Germany, 10 percent Russia, 9 percent United Kingdom, and 23 percent other countries.[18] Russia has been a major supplier of aircraft. European countries have been major suppliers for the navy.

Military Education and Training

The Military Academy (Akademi TNI) in Magelang, Central Java, has been the principal training ground for TNI officers since its establishment in 1957.

18. *SIPRI Yearbook 2004*, from Widjajanto (2005, p. 20).

Table A-2. *Foreign Procurement of Military Equipment, 1999–2003*

Source country	Value (U.S. dollars)	Percent of total
Russia	274	36
United Kingdom	226	29
France	121	16
Germany	74	10
United States	29	4
Netherlands	21	3
Other	26	3
Total	769	100

Source: *SIPRI Yearbook 2004*, from Widjajanto (2005, p. 20).

Akademi TNI feeds cadets completing their first year to the Naval Academy in Surabaya, East Java, and the Air Force Academy in Yogyakarta, while army cadets continue their education in Magelang. The three academies graduate 900–1,000 officers a year after a three-year course of study.

The TNI's principal midcareer training establishment is SESKOTNI, the Armed Forces Staff and Command School in Bandung, West Java. The navy and the air force have separate staff and command schools in Jakarta. LEMHANAS, the National Resilience Institute, specializes in training senior officers and includes study tours to foreign countries in its program.

Methodology for Estimating the Gross Revenue and Net Income of the TNI's Off-Budget Activities

Note: Figures are in billions of rupiah unless otherwise indicated.

A. Business activities

1. Formal business activities

First cut

Gross revenue from all business activities of the TNI and National Police in 2003[a]	1,000
After assuming a National Police share of 20 percent	800
Gross revenue, assuming 60 percent comes from formal businesses	500
Net income, assuming a 20 percent rate of profit	100
After assuming a 15 percent decline (without inflation adjustment) from 2003 to 2006:	
++ Gross revenue in 2006	420
++ Net income in 2006	80

Cross-check

"Book value" of TNI business units on December 2006 list, end-2004	1,500
Gross revenue of these units (equal to book value) in 2004	1,500
Gross revenue after assuming a 10 percent decline from 2004 to 2006	1,350
Net income, assuming a 20 percent rate of profit	270

Estimated ranges for formal business activities
Gross revenue: Rp 420 billion to 1.35 trillion
Net income: Rp 80 billion to 270 billion

a. Source: Van Zorge and others (2003, pp. 10–11).

2. Informal business activities
First cut

"Security services": gross revenue of TNI and National Police for ExxonMobil and Freeport-McMoRan in 2003[b]	70–90
After assuming a National Police share of 30 percent	50–60
After assuming other clients account for 25 percent of total	67–80
After assuming loss of ExxonMobil and Freeport income in 2006	10–20
Security services net income, after assuming gross revenue and net income are the same	10–20
Commercialization of assets: gross revenue from Carrefour lease in 2006	5
After assuming equivalent of 10–20 similar arrangements	50–100
After assuming additional short-term rental income	10–20
Commercialization of assets net income, after assuming gross revenue and net income are the same	60–120
Combined gross revenue and net income for informal business activities	70–140

Cross-check

Total off-budget income of TNI in 2003[c]	800
After assuming Rp 500 billion (60 percent) was generated by formal business activities and Rp 180 billion (25 percent) by illegal activities	120
After assuming a decline of 15 percent from 2003 to 2006	100
Gross revenue and net income for informal business activities after doubling to establish high end of range	100–200

Estimated range for informal business activities

Gross revenue and net income:	70–200

3. Illegal business activities
First cut

Total off-budget income of TNI in 2003[d]	800
After assuming Rp 500 billion (60 percent) was generated by formal business activities and Rp 120 billion (25 percent) by informal business activities	180
After assuming a 30 percent decline from 2003 to 2006	120
Gross revenue and net income for informal business activities after doubling to establish high end of range	120–240

b. Source for ExxonMobil, Van Zorge and others (2003, p. 14); for Freeport-McMoRan, see Jane Perlez and Raymond Bonner, "The Cost of Gold, The Hidden Payroll: Below a Mountain of Wealth, a River of Waste," *New York Times*, December 27, 2005.

c. Source: Van Zorge and others (2003, pp. 10–11), after subtracting National Police share (see formal business section).

d. Source: Van Zorge and others (2003, pp. 10–11), after subtracting the National Police share (see formal business section).

Estimated range for illegal business activities
Gross revenue and net income: 120–240

Recapitulation

(billions of rupiah)	Gross revenue	Net income
From formal business activities:	420–1,350	80–270
From informal business activities:	70–200	70–200
From illegal business activities:	120–240	120–240
All business activities:	610–1,790	270–710
In millions of dollars	63–185	27–73

B. Other income-generating activities

Gifts

Budget allocation for procurement of goods, services, and capital equipment, 2006	16.1 trillion
Gross revenue and net income, assuming gifts equivalent to 2.5–5.0 percent	400 billion to 800 billion

Procurement commissions

Budget allocation for procurement of goods, services, and capital equipment, 2006	16.1 trillion
Gross revenue and net income, assuming procurement commissions equivalent to 5–10 percent	800 billion to 1,600 billion

Recapitulation

Gross revenue and net income from gifts	400 billion to 800 billion
Gross revenue and net income from procurement commissions	800 billion to 1,600 billion
All other income-generating activities	1.2 trillion to 2.4 trillion

C. Total net income and operational vs. nonoperational spending

Net income from business activities, 2006	270 billion to 710 billion
Assuming 40 percent spent for operational purposes	108 billion to 272 billion
Net income from other income-generating activities, 2006	1.2 trillion to 2.4 trillion
Assuming 25 percent spent for operational purposes	300 billion to 600 billion
Total net income spent for operational purposes	408 billion to 872 billion
In dollars	42 million to 91 million

References

Anggoro, Kusnanto. 2001. "Harta, Singgasana dan Pedang." In *Military without Militarism: Suara dari Daerah,* edited by Anas S. Machfudz and Jaleswari Pramodawardhani. Jakarta: LIPI.

Anwar, Dewi Fortuna. 2001. *Negotiating and Consolidating Democratic Civilian Control of the Indonesian Military.* Occasional Papers, Politics and Security Series 4. Honolulu: East-West Center.

Arifianto, Alex. 2004. "Social Security Reform in Indonesia: An Analysis of the National Social Security Bill (RUU Jamsosnas)." Working Paper. Jakarta: SMERU Institute.

Basri, Faisal H. 2001. "ABRI dan Bisnis." In *Military without Militarism: Suara dari Daerah,* edited by Anas S. Machfudz and Jaleswari Pramodawardhani. Jakarta: (LIPI).

Bhakti, Ikrar Nusa. 2003. "Kendala dan Peluang Reformasi Internal TNI." In *Evaluasi Reformasi TNI (1998–2003),* edited by Sri Yanuarti. Jakarta: LIPI.

Chrisnandi, Yuddy. 2005. *Reformasi TNI: Perspektif Baru Hubungan Sipil-Militer di Indonesia.* Jakarta: Lembaga Penelitian, Pendidikan, dan Penerangan Ekonomi dan Sosial (LP3ES).

Crouch, Harold. 1975/76. "Generals and Business in Indonesia." *Pacific Affairs* 48 (Winter): 519–40.

Davidsen, Soren, Vishnu Juwono, and David G. Timberman. 2006. *Curbing Corruption in Indonesia, 2004–2006: A Survey of National Policies and Approaches.* Washington: United States–Indonesia Society (USINDO) and CSIS.

Dehqanzada, Yahya A., and Ann M. Florini. 2000. "Secrets for Sale: How Commercial Satellite Imagery Will Change the World." Washington: Carnegie Endowment for International Peace. Photocopy.

Fathoni, A. 2005. *Sinergi Koperasi—Jilad 1.* Jakarta: Primkopau Mabes TNI AU.

Friend, Theodore. 2003. *Indonesian Destinies.* Harvard University Press.

Government of Indonesia, Ministry of Defense. 2003. *Defending the Country Entering the 21st Century.* Jakarta.

———. 2006. "Indonesian National Defense Forces' (TNI) Reformation, Readiness, Law and Business." Presentation at USINDO. Washington, April 25.

Government of Indonesia, National Police. 2004. *Indonesian National Police Today.* Jakarta.

Hafidz, Tatik S. 2006. *Fading Away? The Political Role of the Army in Indonesia's Transition to Democracy, 1998–2001.* Monograph 8. Singapore: Institute of Defence and Strategic Studies.

Haseman, John B. 2006. "Indonesian Military Reform: More than a Human Rights Issue." In *Southeast Asian Affairs 2006,* edited by Daljit Singh and Larraine C. Salazar. Singapore: Institute of Southeast Asian Studies.

Haseman, John B., and Eduardo Lachica. 2005. *Toward a Stronger U.S.-Indonesia Security Relationship.* Washington: USINDO.

Haseman, John B., and Angel Rabasa. 2002. *The Military and Democracy in Indonesia: Challenges, Politics, and Power.* Santa Monica, Calif.: Rand.

Human Rights Watch. 2006. *Too High A Price: The Human Rights Cost of the Indonesian Military's Economic Activities.* Vol. 18, no. 5(C).

International Crisis Group. 2000. "Indonesia: Keeping the Military under Control." Asia Report 9. Jakarta.

———. 2001a. "Indonesia: National Police Reform." Asia Report 13. Jakarta.

———. 2001b. "Indonesia: Next Steps in Military Reform." Asia Report 24. Jakarta.

International Monetary Fund (IMF). 2006. *Indonesia: Report on Observance of Standards and Codes—Fiscal Transparency Module.* Country Report 06/330. Washington.

Iswandi. 1998. *Bisnis Militer Orde Baru: Keterlibatan ABRI dalam Bidang Ekonomi dan Pengaruhannya terhadap Pembentukan Rezim Otoriter.* Bandung: Pernerbit P.T. Remaja Rosdakarya.

Jamaluddin, J. M. November 2006. "TNI: Towards a More Balanced Force." *Asian Defence Journal,* pp. 17–21.

Lachica, Eduardo, and others. 2004. *Enhancing the U.S.-Indonesian Security Relationship: An Opportunity Not to Be Missed.* Washington: USINDO.

Lowry, Robert. 1996. *The Armed Forces of Indonesia.* St. Leonards, Australia: Allen & Unwin.

McBeth, John. 2002. "The Army's Dirty Business." *Far Eastern Economic Review,* November 7.

McCulloch, Lesley. 2000. "Trifungsi: The Role of the Indonesian Military in Business." Paper presented at the International Conference on Soldiers in Business: Military as an Economic Actor. Jakarta, October 17–19.

McVey, Ruth. 1971. "The Post-Revolution Transformation of the Indonesian Army (Part I)." *Indonesia.* Modern Indonesia Project. Cornell University.

————. 1972. "The Post-Revolution Transformation of the Indonesian Army (Part II)." *Indonesia*. Modern Indonesia Project. Cornell University.

Mietzner, Marcus. 2003. "Business as Usual? The Indonesian Armed Forces and Local Politics in the Post-Suharto Era." In *Local Power and Politics in Indonesia: Democratization and Decentralization*, edited by Edward Aspinall and Greg Fealy. Singapore: Institute of Southeast Asian Studies (ISEAS).

Nunberg, Barbara, and others. 2000. "Priorities for Civil Service Reform in Indonesia." East Asia Poverty Reduction and Economic Management Unit (EASPR) paper. Washington: World Bank.

Nurhasim, Moch., ed. 2005. *Practices of Military Business: Experiences from Indonesia, Burma, Philippines, and South Korea*. Jakarta: Friedrich-Ebert-Stiftung and Ridep Institute.

Obidzinski, Krystof, Agus Andrianto, and Chandra Wijaya. 2006. *Timber Smuggling in Indonesia: Critical or Overstated Problem*. Bogor: Center for Forestry Research.

O'Rourke, Kevin. 2002. *Reformasi: The Struggle for Power in Post-Soeharto Indonesia*. Sydney: Allen & Unwin.

Percival, Bronson. 2005. *Indonesia and the United States: Shared Interests in Maritime Security*. Washington: USINDO.

Pramodhawardani, Jaleswari. 2004. "Transparensi, Akuntabilitas, dan Kontrol dalam Pembiayaan Pertahan: Problem dan Rekomendasi." Working Paper for the Ministry of Defense. Jakarta.

Rachmatarwata, Isa. 2004. "Indonesia Pension System: Where to Go?" Paper prepared for the International Conference on Pensions in Asia: Incentives, Compliance and Their Role in Retirement. Tokyo, February 23–24.

Rieffel, Alexis, and Aninda S. Wirjasuputra. 1972. "Military Enterprises." *Bulletin of Indonesian Economic Studies* 9 (July): 104–08.

Rieffel, Lex. 2004. "Indonesia's Quiet Revolution." *Foreign Affairs* 83 (September/October): 98–110.

Rinakit, Sukardi. 2004. "The Role of the Military in the Future: From Critical Support to Hegemony?" In *Meneropong Indonesia 2020: Pemikiran dan Masalah Kebijakan*, edited by Soegeng Sarjadi and Sukardi Rinakit. Jakarta: Soegeng Sarjadi Syndicated.

————. 2005. *The Indonesian Military after the New Order*. Singapore: Institute of Southeast Asian Studies.

Robison, Richard. 1986. *Indonesia: The Rise of Capital*. Sydney: Allen & Unwin.

Robison, Richard, and Vedi R. Hadiz. 2004. *Reorganising Power in Indonesia: The Politics of Oligarchy in an Age of Markets*. London: RoutledgeCurzon.

Said, Salim. 2006a. *Soeharto's Armed Forces: Problems of Civil-Military Relations in Indonesia*. Jakarta: Pustaka Sinar Harapan.

————. 2006b. *Legitimizing Military Rule: Indonesian Armed Forces Ideology, 1958–2000*. Jakarta: Pustaka Sinar Harapan. (Also published in 2002 in Indonesian as *Tumbuh dan Tumbangan Dwifungsi: Perkembangan Militer Indonesia 1958–2000.* Jakarta: Aksara Karunia.)

Samego, Indria, and others. 1998. *Bila ABRI Berbisnis: Buku Pertama yang Menyingkap Data dan Kasus Penyimpangan dalam Praktik Bisnis Kalangan Militer.* Bandung: Penerbit Mizan.

———. 2002. *Anatomi Kekuatan TNI sebagai Alat Pertahanan Negara.* Jakarta: LIPI.

Schwarz, Adam. 1994. *A Nation in Waiting: Indonesia in the 1990s.* Boulder, Colo.: Westview Press.

Sebastian, Leonard C. 2006. *Realpolitik Ideology: Indonesia's Use of Military Force.* Singapore: Institute of Southeast Asian Studies.

Singh, Bilveer. 1996. *Dwifungsi ABRI: Asal-usul, Aktualisasi dan Implikasinya bagi Stabilitas dan Pembangunan.* Jakarta: P.T. Gramedia.

———. 2001. "The Indonesian Military Business Complex: Origins, Course and Future." Working Paper 354. Australian National University, Strategic and Defence Studies Centre.

Smith, Rupert. 2005. *The Utility of Force: The Art of War in the Modern World.* London: Allen Lane.

Steadman, David, and Lloyd Kendall. 2005. *Civil Service Reforms at the Regional Level—Opportunities and Constraints.* Washington: World Bank.

Stockholm International Peace Research Institute (SIPRI). 2004. *SIPRI Yearbook 2004.*

Sudarsono, Juwono. 2004. "Military Reform and Defense Planning: A Top Priority for Indonesia's Next Administration." In *Indonesian Voices: Hopes and Concerns for the Future,* Tenth Anniversary Collection. Washington: USINDO.

Sukadis, Beni, and Eric Hendra (eds.). 2005. *Toward Professional TNI: TNI Business Restructuring.* Jakarta: Friedrich-Ebert-Stiftung and Lembaga Studi Pertahanan dan Studi Strategis Indonesia (LESPERSSI).

Sukma, Rizal. 2003. "Military and Politics in Post-Suharto Indonesia." In *Indonesia Matters: Diversity, Unity, and Stability in Fragile Times,* edited by Thang D. Nguyen and Frank-Jurgen Richter. Singapore: Times Media Private.

———. 2006. "Mengatur Pertahanan: Kajian Atas Kerganka Legal Reformasi Pertahanan Indonesia." Draft chapter for CSIS-led study, "Defense in the 21st Century." Jakarta.

Tim Penelitian. 2004. *Ketika Moncong Senjata Ikut Berniaga: Laporan Penelitian Keterlibatan Militer Dalam Bisnis di Bojonegoro, Boven Digoel dan Poso.* Jakarta: KontraS (Executive Summary in English: *Research Team. When Gun Point Joins the Trade: Military Business Involvement in Bojonegoro, Boven Digoel and Poso*).

United Nations Support Facility for Indonesian Recovery (UNSFIR). 2005. *Membangun TNI yang Profesional sebagai Pelaksana Fungsi Pertahanan Nasional dalam rangka Konsolidasi Demokrasi.* Prosidang Lokakarya di Jakarta pada 6–7 Oktober 2004. Jakarta.

United States–Indonesia Society (USINDO). 2004. *Indonesian Voices: Hopes and Concerns for the Future.* Tenth Anniversary Collection. Washington.

Van Zorge, Heffernan & Associates. 2003. "The Tentacles of the Octopus: The Business Interests of the TNI and Police." *Van Zorge Report on Indonesia,* vol. V/9 (July 16).

Widjaja, Mas. 2004. *Dukungan Anggaran Pertahanan.* Makalah disaji pada Lokakarya Membangun TNI Yang Profesional Sebagai Pelaksana Fungsi Pertahanan Nasional dalam rangka Sumbangan TNI Bagi Konsolodasi Demokrasi. Direktorat Jenderal Perencanaan System Pertahanan, Departmen Pertahanan. Jakarta, September 28–29, 2004.

Widjajanto, Andi. 2005. "Kompleksitas Ekonomi Pertahanan Indonesia." Draft chapter for Centre for Strategic and International Studies (CSIS) project, "Defense in the 21st Century." Jakarta.

Widjajanto, Andi, and Edy Prasetyono. 2006. "The Territorial Command: Indonesia's Defense Strategy and Posture in the Future." Draft chapter for Centre for Strategic and International Studies (CSIS) project, "Defense in the 21st Century." Jakarta.

Widjojo, Agus, Andi Widjajanto, and Andre Sigit. 2005. *Draft Rekomendasi Buku Putih Kibijakan Reformasi TNI.* Jakarta: United Nations Support Facility for Indonesian Recovery (UNSFIR).

Widoyoko, Danang, and others. 2002. *Military Business in Search for Legitimacy.* Jakarta: Indonesian Corruption Watch.

Wise, William. 2005. *Indonesia's War on Terror.* Washington: USINDO.

Working Group on Security Sector Reform in Indonesia. 2005. "Naskah Akademik: Pengambilalihan Aktivitas Bisnis Militer." Jakarta: Indonesian Institute. Photocopy.

World Bank. 2000. *Indonesia: Accelerating Recovery in Uncertain Times.* Prepared for the Consultative Group on Indonesia. Jakarta.

———. 2003a. *Combating Corruption in Indonesia: Enhancing Accountability for Development.* Washington.

———. 2003b. *CGI Brief: Beyond Macroeconomic Stability.* Report 27374-IND. Jakarta.

———. 2006. *Indonesia: Investing for Growth and Recovery.* Report 35423-IND. Prepared for the Consultative Group for Indonesia. Jakarta.

Yunanto, S., and others. 2005. "The Structure of Indonesian Military Business: When Will It End?" In *Practices of Military Business: Experiences from Indonesia, Burma, Philippines, and South Korea,* edited by Moch. Nurhasim. Jakarta: Friedrich-Ebert-Stiftung and Ridep Institute.

Index